Monkey Business

37 Better Business Practices Learned Through Monkeys

Comments on the book

"An experience of Oneness with nature is a fundamental human longing. As more of us live more removed from nature's cycles and from growing and harvesting our own food we grasp for glimpses of nature in our interactions with the animals who are part of our lives. In this book, Heather Wandell has carefully observed her monkey friends and is able, through them, to remind each of us of basic wisdom practices—ways of living that are obvious in nature—and obscured for many of us with too much intellect and too little raw capacity to observe. Heather and her friends are a call for readers to recapture our capacity to be One with Nature."

—Bob Duggan, President, Tai Sophia Institute, www.tai.edu

"Monkey Business is so uplifting. Your comments make me reflect. You have a special talent to see possibilities for making us better."

—Patricia Storch, General and Elder Law Attorney, Former Assistant Attorney General

"These wonderful life lessons learned from monkeys and skillfully applied to us less hairy ones contain a beautiful, heartfelt, recurring theme. Proceed in all you do with Gratitude, Awe, and Reverence for All that Is. If you believe these principle do not apply to business ... I'd guess you haven't really tried or perhaps are trying too hard. Try easier."

—Mark Iberg, CEO & Chief Bottle Washer, LCServices, http://lcsvs.com

"Heather Wandell's "Monkey Business" series has added feelings of serenity, decency, and thoughtfulness for others (human and nonhuman alike) to my rather bleak, activist-oriented, global warming newspaper. We cover a lot of bad news about the destruction of the planet but the only way to really change the outcome is by changing the human heart and spirit. Heather's stories help us with that transformation; they help soften our hearts and bring us closer to Most High God."

—Iona Conner, Publisher of the *Order of the Earth* newspaper

Monkey Business

37 Better Business Practices
Learned Through Monkeys

Heather A. Wandell, MA, CLL

OPEN BOOK
EDITIONS
A Berrett–Koehler Partner

Monkey Business
37 Better Business Practices Learned Through Monkeys

iUniverse books may be ordered through booksellers or by contacting:

iUniverse
1663 Liberty Drive
Bloomington, IN 47403
www.iuniverse.com
1-800-Authors (1-800-288-4677)

ISBN: 978-1-4759-1175-6 (sc)
ISBN: 978-1-4759-1177-0 (hc)
ISBN: 978-1-4759-1176-3 (e)

Library of Congress Control Number: 2012906552

Printed in the United States of America

iUniverse rev. date: 6/18/2012

Contents

Acknowledgments vii
Cast of Characters xi
Introduction 1

Part 1: Creating an Environment Where Possibility Thrives

Chapter 1: My Space 17
Chapter 2: Movement 21
Chapter 3: Metaphors 24
Chapter 4: Gardens and Grace 29
Chapter 5: Guilty 33
Chapter 6: Alternate Role 36

Part 2: Acknowledging Our Shared Humanity

Chapter 7: Hugs 43
Chapter 8: Impermanence 48
Chapter 9: Feeling Important 52
Chapter 10: Presence 55
Chapter 11: Excessive Celebration 58

Part 3: Getting Along

Chapter 12: Silence 65
Chapter 13: Guests 69
Chapter 14: Without Sam 73
Chapter 15: The Patsy 76
Chapter 16: The Donkey 80
Chapter 17: Declaration 84

Part 4: Communicating with Awareness

Chapter 18: Being Disturbed 89
Chapter 19: Thief 92
Chapter 20: Do or Do Not 96
Chapter 21: Both-And 99
Chapter 22: The Power of No 104
Chapter 23: Uh-Uh 107
Chapter 24: Simply Speaking 112

Part 5: Evolving Our Business Paradigm

Chapter 25: Certitudes 119
Chapter 26: Enough 123
Chapter 27: Security 127
Chapter 28: One Thing 130
Chapter 29: Ring-Around-the-Rosy 133
Chapter 30: Flow 137
Chapter 31: Associates 142

Part 6: Opening to Optimism

Chapter 32: Smile 147
Chapter 33: The Key 150
Chapter 34: Bananas 154
Chapter 35: Favorite Places 158
Chapter 36: Perseverance 162
Chapter 37: Quit Complaining! 166
Chapter 38: Privilege 170
In Memory 173

Acknowledgements

I am deeply grateful to Colleen Layton-Robbins, my selfless friend, for the gift of a second chance at life, which you have given to thousands who have come to your door. I have watched your heart break a thousand times when you have helped one, who was injured too badly, to cross over. I have seen you celebrate the lives of those who have thrived under your care and are ready to return to their natural homes in the wild. I have seen you love and nurture primates who have come to you because of poor human judgment and serve them until the end of their days. Thank you for allowing me to be a part of this mission, for encouraging me to write my column and this book, and for permission to use your photos.

Thank you to Scott Robbins for loving and supporting your wife and my friend, Colleen, in this mission. For many years, you have worked hard during the day as a mechanic, coming home to mow lawns, repair fences, clean cages, feed little mouths, and do whatever is most pressing that day.

Thank you to all the dedicated volunteers of Frisky's Wildlife and Primate Sanctuary, who come after work or on their days off, or who have made this their work, because all life matters to you.

Thank you to Reverend Nancy Stepp, head minister at the Center for Spiritual Living, Laurel for your loving support and belief in me.

Thank you to Roz Trieber, a dear friend, author, and speaker, who believed I could do this and helped me with resources along the way, even though she was struggling with cancer. Roz has made her transition into the nonphysical realm, but I know she is still cheering me on.

Thank you to Bob Duggan, president and co-founder of the Tai Sophia Institute for the Healing Arts in Laurel, MD, for being my teacher.

Thank you to Dianne Connelly, co-founder and chancellor of the Tai Sophia Institute in Laurel, MD, for being my teacher.

Thank you to my husband, Robert "Bob" Wandell II, for being my tech-man, sounding board, and love.

Thank you to my daughter, Morgan Wandell, for your graphic design on the front and back cover—you are amazing. www.morgan-wandell.com.

Thank you to Judy Stevenson for helping me to stick to my weekly goals when the editing task seemed daunting.

Thank you to my editors, Gordon Styles (my wonderful dad) and Dana Knighten (InWord Journeys), for helping me take *Monkey Business* from a monthly column to a book.

Thank you to my mom, Janet Styles, for always thinking my writing deserved an A, even when it didn't.

Thank you to my son, Bradley Wandell, for being the reason I went to Frisky's in the first place.

Thank you to Eric Mettala, PhD, for being my earliest coach in the beginnings of the monthly column.

Thank you to Terri Oliver, RScP; Jane Reilly, RScP; Joanna Clark, RScP; and Reverend Annette Cameron for your spiritual guidance and affirmative prayer treatments for Frisky's.

Thank you to Laura Mueller, my acupuncturist, who kept me on track.

Thank you to the Simian Society of America for your support in printing my monthly columns in your magazine for two years.

Thank you to all who have read the column, bought the CD, and/or given me the encouragement that these stories have served you in some way.

Thank you to all the authors who gave me their blessings in allowing me to quote them in my book. To the 20 percent of you I could not reach or never heard back from, I ask for your blessing. Your magnificent words and thoughts have, are, and will be serving many beings, both human and nonhuman.

Cast of Characters

I have included a "cast of characters" listing those you'll meet in the pages of this book as a handy reference to help you remember who's who as you read.

Keep in mind that these characters are real—and they really *are* characters! This book is not a work of fiction; the stories included here are all true. All of the monkeys mentioned in *Monkey Business* actually reside or resided at Frisky's Wildlife and Primate Sanctuary, Inc., in Woodstock, Maryland, and all of the humans mentioned are also real.

You'll notice that I didn't put the humans by themselves in a separate "cast"—after all, we're all primates!

Angel
Mona guenon monkey, female
Born 10/12/98, arrived at Frisky's 11/24/98

Loves to bounce, especially on her bouncing toy horse. Gives Winnie the Pooh's friend Tigger a run for his money.

Babee
Weeper capuchin monkey, female
Born 9/23/95, arrived at Frisky's 10/23/95

Likes sharing meals with Colleen. Loves her swings. Enjoys grooming her companion, Willie. When Bonnie, a volunteer, arrives with special treats, Babee runs back and forth and then up to her bedbox, where she figures Willie cannot steal her treat.

Bob Duggan

Human, male

President and co-founder of the Tai Sophia Institute in Laurel, Maryland. Acupuncturist, teacher, and author. Focuses on "What is possible? What are the implications of what we say and do for the future?"

Bimbee

Weeper capuchin monkey, female

Born 11/15/71, arrived at Frisky's 4/1/2000

Loves frozen yogurt as a bedtime snack and will bang on the bars of her enclosure with a spoon until you bring it to her. You can tell what time of day it is by Bimbee. She "screams for ice cream"!

Cindy-Lou

Gothic squirrel monkey, female

Born 9/15/91, arrived at Frisky's 2/19/97

Loves playing with baby rattles and eating Pasta Pick-Ups. Loves to lick the yogurt off the strawberry yogurt pretzels that volunteer Bonnie brings her every week. She tends to be shy.

CoCo

Rhesus macaque monkey, male

Born 9/15/86, arrived at Frisky's 9/23/96

Loves blankets and mirrors. Is also Frisky's resident "room monitor"—watches everyone and gives them the dickens if they get out of line.

Cocoa

Gothic squirrel monkey, female

Born 8/15/96, arrived at Frisky's 4/1/97

Loves caramel-colored stuffed toys to carry around and cuddle. We think it's because they match her coloring.

Colleen Layton-Robbins

Human, female

Master wildlife rehabilitator, founder, and president of Frisky's Wildlife and Primate Sanctuary (founded in 1970). Believes that every life deserves a second chance. Has dedicated her life and home to thousands who have crossed her doorstep.

Darrow

Gothic squirrel monkey, female

Born 7/10/98, arrived at Frisky's 10/13/02

Quiet and shy unless you offer food. Loves Pasta Pick-Ups. Shares an enclosure with Darwin. She and Darwin both lived in New York City originally.

Darwin

Gothic squirrel monkey, male

Born 7/10/97, arrived at Frisky's 10/13/03

Loves being "Macho Man." Makes himself big and tall and tries to mark his territory when you come near. Squeals loudly himself, but does not tolerate noise from others. He weighs about 2.5 lbs. Shares enclosure with Darrow. Both are from New York City.

Dawson

Java macaque monkey, male

Born 4/25/01, arrived at Frisky's 9/16/01

He's a "tail teaser"—only offers his tail outside of the enclosure for those he trusts. Hides his privates when people are looking at him.

Diana

Vervet guenon monkey, female

Born 7/2/91, arrived at Frisky's 7/5/97

Enjoys stuffed animals. Is the most cooperative monkey when it comes to cleaning her enclosure. Will go easily from indoors to outdoors and vice versa.

Dianne Connelly

Human, female

Chancellor and co-founder of the Tai Sophia Institute in Laurel, Maryland. Acupuncturist, teacher, and author. Gifted with language, acupuncture needles, and the human spirit.

Gizmo

Rhesus macaque monkey, male

Born 9/15/89, arrived at Frisky's 10/15/89

Loves storybooks and being read to. Enjoys eating pizza with Scott. The first monkey to arrive at Frisky's.

Grisha

White-headed marmoset monkey, male

Born 10/15/05, arrived at Frisky's 10/17/07

Loves looking at himself in the mirror—from all angles. Just loves to be noticed and admired by all.

Isadora

Black and white capuchin monkey, female

Born 11/22/96, arrived at Frisky's 5/30/01

Loves being sung to and playing Simon Says. Will imitate your movements and sounds.

Jackie

Vervet guenon monkey, female

Born 10/15/84, arrived at Frisky's 1/13/01

Loves being surrounded by lots of stuffed animals. Grooms them and mothers them as if they were real babies. She loves when you ask about her "babies." She will pick them up and start "talking" about them. Has one little elephant that you can tell she favors. It is very worn out and loved.

Jamie

Bonnet macaque monkey, male

Born 4/6/97, arrived at Frisky's 4/6/99

Was "arrested" along with his owner in a barroom brawl that was started by the humans. Brought to Frisky's by the authorities. Loves his hammock. Sucks on his fingers and ponders the world.

Johnny

Weeper capuchin monkey, male

Born 7/6/97, arrived at Frisky's 7/14/97

Biological mother had twins and couldn't care for Johnny, who needed twenty-four-hour care. Loves playful teasing—especially teasing Willie.

Keith Gold, DVM

Human, male

Veterinarian at Chadwell Animal Hospital, Abingdon, Maryland; director of Luna's House, a nonprofit that finds homes for abandoned animals. Is Frisky's primary veterinarian for monkey and other exotic animal care. Believes "there is a place on this earth for every animal."

Kiko

Rhesus macaque monkey, male

Born 3/6/95, arrived at Frisky's 1/27/99

Likes throwing things up in the air and seeing his toys bounce off the walls. Enjoys balls. Loves mashed sweet potato and apple juice in a bottle. Pictured on the cover.

Lucy

Vervet guenon monkey, female

Born approximately 3/15/07, arrived at Frisky's 9/7/07

Was found in the garage of a vacant house. Loves her teddy bears and can't stand to see them drop on the floor. Will immediately pick up any toys Diana drops.

Michael Cranfield, DVM

Human, male

Director of veterinary care at The Maryland Zoo in Baltimore; director of the Mountain Gorilla Veterinary Project (MGVP) in Rwanda and Uganda. Committed to MGVP's mission to help ensure these gentle gorillas' quality of life and future existence through health care, research, and public education.

Mr. Bojangles

See "In Memory"

Nicole

See "In Memory"

Nikki

Gothic squirrel monkey, female

Born 12/22/86, arrived at Frisky's 6/29/2001

Loves baby rattles and snuggling in blankets. Enjoys having Colleen scratch her back when all is quiet.

Oogie

Cinnamon capuchin monkey, female

Born 10/28/91, arrived at Frisky's 12/24/96

Loves being sung to and danced with by her favorite people. Enjoys being tickled. Beware to first-time visitors—she will fling whatever she can find at those she does not know.

Patsy

See "In Memory"

Rachelle

See "In Memory"

Reverend Nancy Stepp

Human, female

Senior minister of the Center for Spiritual Living in Laurel (CSLL). Teacher of Science of Mind principles. Has a way of teaching with heart, humor, insight, clarity, and passion. She is a great storyteller, offering tales to deliver a spiritual message.

Sam

See "In Memory"

Scott Robbins

Human, male

Husband of Colleen Layton-Robbins and vice president of Frisky's Wildlife and Primate Sanctuary, Inc. Mechanic by day, lawn maintenance and animal care provider by night. In previous years, he was a race car driver. Now he races around the sanctuary to get things done.

Scotty, Jr.

See "In Memory"

Squeaky

See "In Memory"

Steve Wilson

Human, male

Founder of World Laughter Tour and Good-Hearted Living Practices. Psychologist, author, teacher, and speaker. World Laughter Tour recognizes Steve as "Cheerman of the Bored." Has inspired thousands around the world to laugh more for improved life experience.

Vito

Weeper capuchin monkey, male

Born 8/2/96, arrived at Frisky's 8/6/06

Loves hugging his teddy bears and playing peekaboo with his sheets. He is very affectionate. A sweet disposition.

Willie

Wedge-capped capuchin monkey, male

Born 8/15/89, arrived at Frisky's 2/9/95

Loves women—he is a flirt. Enjoys soap operas on TV. Shares an enclosure with Babee. Will hold your hand and just squeal with delight. Makes you feel loved.

Yoo

Capuchin monkey, female

Born 9/14/99, arrived at Frisky's 10/14/99

Spent the first several months of her life in an incubator. Has the most precious little face, makes heart-melting eye contact. Loves quiet time with Colleen.

Zoey

See "In Memory"

Colleen Layton-Robbins and Scott Robbins

Introduction

Oogie sobbed with abandon the day we lost little Cindy Lou. She was the first one to know it, as their enclosures had been catty-corner to each other for the last several years.

Colleen, the manager of the sanctuary and primary caregiver to these monkeys, woke up to the saddest sound she had ever heard coming from her cinnamon capuchin monkey. Little Cindy Lou, a gothic squirrel monkey, had passed away just before sunrise. After removing Cindy Lou's lifeless body from her enclosure, Colleen cuddled Oogie for two hours, trying to console her. But exhausted and grief-stricken herself over the loss, she called in Janice, the administrator for Frisky's Wildlife and Primate Sanctuary, to see if her visit could console Oogie. Janice's presence did help Oogie, as a visit from a friend after losing a loved one would be a comfort to any of us.

Unaware of all of this, I arrived at Frisky's that morning to say good-bye before I flew back to Abu Dhabi for the final months of my husband's two-year work contract in the United Arab Emirates. When Colleen answered the door, her eyes were swollen and the look on her face made me freeze, bracing myself to hear bad news. I'm not sure a second even passed before I broke into tears. I embraced Colleen, and then Janice, and listened as they let the events of the morning unfold.

I could hear a few faint sounds coming from Oogie in the other room. I offered to go visit with her, if they thought it would be of some help. Colleen told me that it might be worth a try. So I began to sing to Oogie. She was quiet and then offered me her tail, a ritual of our friendship.

We were all there for each other that morning, one being helping another being to get through an event that brought us great suffering.

The stories in the following chapters will offer many opportunities for you to see the similarities in behavior between human primates and nonhuman primates (monkeys). Each story compares the monkeys' behavior to a workplace behavior and offers a lesson at the end. To more fully experience the lessons offered in this book, I encourage you to read the entire introduction first. It will become clear that these lessons and practices are meant for personal use as well as business use.

In January 2004, after much deliberation and many excuses about "why this isn't the right time," I enrolled in the Applied Healing Arts Program at the Tai Sophia Institute in Laurel, Maryland. Tai Sophia is a graduate school accredited by the Middle States Commission on Higher Education (MSCHE), offering master's degrees in acupuncture, nutrition and integrative health, therapeutic herbalism, and transformative leadership and social change.

The last is the new name for the program I was enrolled in, and perhaps a better description than its previous name. In this program, we learned to use words and practices as our "needle" to transform emotional suffering, instead of the actual needle that is used in acupuncture. Never before had I even entertained the idea of going for my master's degree until this program came to my awareness. But events beyond my knowing were afoot, and all were conspiring in my favor. Fortunately, I was open to noticing the direction in which those events were pointing.

For several years before I actually enrolled at Tai Sophia, people kept showing up in my life who had graduated from the institute or who were currently working on one of the institute's master's degree programs. These people all seemed to have a way of relating to others, and just "being" in general, that seemed different from most. This way of "being" felt really good to be around. There were people in the program who had traveled from all over the country to study at the institute—and here it was just twenty minutes from my home.

I finally took one noncredit class at the institute in January 2003, and I found there the kind of conversation and thinking that I knew I wanted to be involved in for the rest of my life.

I couldn't have known it then, but enrolling in that master's program was a decision that would change my life. This book is part of that change.

Tai Sophia's Influence

About the time I started at Tai Sophia, my oldest child was in high school. Those years, 2002 through 2004, were extremely traumatic for our whole family. The county school system was not supportive of a child who didn't thrive within their narrow parameters, and we felt like we were drowning. Our child had a brilliant, creative mind, and the school system tried to fit her into their mold. It wasn't working. We had to take what, at the time, felt like life-saving action, and all on our own. As I researched and put into place the programs that I felt would benefit our child, I also knew that I wanted to change the way that I looked at life and responded to situations.

Up to that point, I had been following all of the accepted "good parent rules": constant questioning, daily invasion of backpacks, insisting on knowing where my children were at every moment—all of the standard popular wisdom about how to parent a teenager. But following all these rules just about destroyed our family.

It was at this point that Tai Sophia changed everything. Over time, the institute, its programs, its staff, and my fellow students helped me learn to look at everything differently—the news, the world, my beliefs and actions, relationships, parenting, health, and our relationship with and responsibility to nature. Today, our daughter is a brilliant and successful young lady. And now I can see that she always has been.

I believe it was no accident that Tai Sophia came into my life at this time. Nor do I believe it was an accident that around this same time, two other great sources of teaching and learning entered my world.

The Center for Spiritual Living and Science of Mind

When I first met Reverend Nancy Stepp, she was the minister at the Center for Spiritual Living in Columbia, Maryland. From her I learned about the Science of Mind (SOM), the principles of which are practiced at the center. Science of Mind teaches that there is a power for good in the universe that each of us can use, and that we create our lives with our words and our thoughts. The universe is a mirror and will reflect life right back at us through our thoughts, words, and actions. And it works. Each of us is a magnet for universal energy, and we can use it *for* or *against* ourselves. We get to choose, so we should make that choice consciously. When Reverend Nancy later moved on to open the Center for Spiritual Living in Laurel, Maryland, in January 2008, I moved right along with her.

Along the way, I discovered that the Center for Spiritual Living's teachings and practices and those of Tai Sophia went hand in hand. Both share the belief that the way we use words has an enormous influence in creating our world. Both teach that by focusing on one steadfast, weekly practice at a time, we have the power to improve our relationships, improve physical and mental health, increase abundance, and reduce unnecessary suffering—the kind of suffering that we create through our own beliefs and way of looking at the world.

Frisky's Wildlife and Primate Sanctuary

In summer 2004, Frisky's Wildlife and Primate Sanctuary in Woodstock, Maryland, came into my life. It brought me twenty-four new nonhuman teachers—monkeys! I had read little bits here and there about Frisky's but did not seem to make a connection until I was looking for a place for my son to do some volunteer work. I felt that he had far too much free time on his hands that summer, and I wanted him to do something constructive, such as being of service in the community. I also hoped he would learn something about nature that he could not learn through books in school.

After about four weeks, he was eager to begin the grueling workouts that come with high school football and leave Frisky's behind. He had discovered that "fecal management" at a wildlife center was not for him. To my surprise, I discovered instead that volunteering at Frisky's just might be right for me.

In those four weeks of dropping off my son and picking him up from the sanctuary, I had grown to admire Colleen Layton-Robbins, the woman who runs the sanctuary. Colleen works tirelessly to save the lives of hundreds of common backyard animals that are brought to her doorstep each year. She has even turned her own home into a sanctuary for these injured, orphaned, and abandoned wild animals and exotic pet give-ups. Colleen believes that all of God's creations deserve a second chance at life, and she had come to recognize back in 1970 that her mission in life was to give it. I had never personally met anyone before who was willing to devote their entire life to a cause—giving up vacations, the normal privacy of a home, family and holiday gatherings, and nights out with her husband or friends, to be in service to the greater cause. Ask Colleen about this and she will honestly tell you, "I don't know what I did to deserve such a wonderful life." I was in awe and still am to this day.

This mission began for Colleen in 1970 in Gettysburg, Pennsylvania, when a family was out for a walk and found four baby rabbits next to the railroad track. The mother rabbit lay dead. The family who found the rabbits wanted to help and thought that Colleen, being of Native American descent, might know what to do. They knocked on her door and asked if she could save them. She took the baby rabbits in, and that was the beginning of Frisky's. Word spread that she could heal injured animals and raise those that were orphaned until they were old enough to go out on their own.

Six-week-old baby Gizmo, a rhesus macaque, was the first monkey to arrive at Frisky's in 1989. Colleen received a series of phone calls from some folks in Cincinnati, Ohio, telling her the plight of this baby monkey who had been rejected by his mother. They wanted to know if she would take him into her sanctuary. After hearing her hesitancy, they played on her emotions and told her that he would die if he did not receive immediate care from a surrogate mother. They also said that he was just too much trouble for them and they were no longer willing to provide care for this baby. Panicked that these people would let this little baby die without care or love, she hopped into her RV with the animals she had in her care at the time and drove straight to Cincinnati. Trying to rationalize her actions in her own mind, she thought if she could raise two boys as a widowed mother living near poverty level, she could handle a baby monkey. When she first laid eyes on baby Gizmo, she knew she could not leave Cincinnati without taking this little guy with her. Once she agreed, they said to her "We need three thousand dollars from you." The truth came out that they were broker/breeders. Living on next to nothing, but always finding a way to make ends meet, she sold her extra truck at home. Colleen has always had a strong faith that GOD will provide her with the resources she needs.

Although it is now illegal to have monkeys as pets in most states, and they may no longer cross state lines, that was not the case in 1989. Gizmo was born into the pet trade. Frisky's became his permanent home. Patsy, a female rhesus macaque and the second nonhuman primate to arrive at the sanctuary, came two years later. Frisky's is now a licensed sanctuary and a permanent home to ex-pet primates.

In 1976, Colleen moved to Elkridge, Maryland, where she continued her mission. Here, she met one volunteer she knew she didn't want to lose—in fact, she appreciated him so much that she married him! Scott Robbins is the amazing man in Colleen's life.

In 1991, Colleen and Scott bought the 3.75 acre farm that is now their home and home to many in need of a second chance. There are very few human comforts at Frisky's—it's the comfort of the animals that matters there. The rooms that in most homes would be a living room and dining room, house enclosures for animals that have special needs. The yard and the outbuildings are also devoted to providing safe, comfortable housing and care for the animals. There are no fees, and there are no paychecks. Everyone at the sanctuary is a volunteer, including Colleen and Scott. Frisky's is a 501(c)3 nonprofit organization. Scott works a day job, and the sanctuary relies on good-hearted donations from the public.

In Jewish folklore, there are thirty-six hidden saints called the Lamed Vov. Unlettered and insignificant, they work at humble trades and pass unnoticed. Because of these anonymous saints, the world continues to exist. In *My Grandfather's Blessings* by Rachel Naomi Remen, MD, Rachel recalls her grandfather telling her the story of these humble saints:

> Only God knows who the Lamed-Vovniks are. Even the Lamed-Vovniks themselves do not know for sure the role they have in the continuation of the world, and no one else knows it either. They respond to suffering, not in order to save the world but simply because the suffering of others touches and matters to them. (p. 352)

In this story, God tells us that he will allow the world to continue as long as at any given time there are a minimum of thirty-six good people in the human race. I believe Colleen and Scott are Lamed-Vovniks. They are simple, hardworking people who take little credit for their magnificent gift to life. They are amazing, and they don't even know it.

Caring for All

"Caring for all" is one of the basic themes woven throughout this book. To me, it means not only caring *for* and *about* other species, but also our own species as well. If we don't treat our own species with respect and kindness, we may have big problems caring for other species. Humans who are angry, neglected, dishonored, and made to feel "less than" often try to take their power back by picking on weaker beings, whether human or nonhuman. So this book is about respecting all and voluntarily adopting practices that reduce human suffering. When we reduce our own suffering, we also reduce the suffering of others as well—*all* others.

You see, when I am unkind, this ripples out to others. If I look down on others and treat them badly, then I am partly responsible for the murder I just read about in the paper. It is as if a part of me pulled that trigger. My unkindness may have rippled out to someone who was on the edge and pushed them over. So, as a daily practice, I choose kindness. Sure, I slip up sometimes. When I am in awareness that I slipped up, I call kindness forth again. Other people's moods are contagious to us. So what mood do you want to infect others with?

I began reading and watching videos on the effect that laughter has on mood and the power it has to connect people. In August 2004, I attended training with World Laughter Tour and became a Certified Laughter Leader (CLL). CLLs are trained to lead playful, therapeutic laughter exercises (movements along with laughter) and positive activity interventions that teach individuals ways to increase their positive thinking, positive affect, and positive behaviors. World Laughter Tour methods draw on positive psychology, social psychology, affective neuroscience, game theory, modern science, and ancient spiritual practices.

In January 2005, I left my job as the marketing director at Winter Growth, an adult day care and assisted living center in Columbia, Maryland, and founded my company, Another Way To See It, LLC. I started my company because of the nagging sense in my gut that I needed to share with my community all the gifts I had received to that point from therapeutic laughter and transformational life practices.

Another Way To See It offers workshops and speaking engagements on healing life practices that transform the way we look at things. These workshops have been presented to hundreds of groups, including hospital employees, lawyers, teachers, senior centers, social workers, and a conference on childhood leukemia. In 2010, Another Way To See It was the recipient of the COGS partnership award. The Coalition of Geriatric Services (COGS) in Howard County, Maryland, presents this annual award to an individual and an organization which, through building partnerships, have made significant contributions to the well-being of the older adult population.

In March 2007, I trained with Steve Wilson to become a trainer with World Laughter Tour. Beginning in January 2009 and ending in the spring of 2010, I trained with Pragito Dove to become a Certified Laughter Meditator. Through steadfast and mindful laughter practices that are not based on joke-telling, I have noticed that upset doesn't stay with me as long. Life shows up much more often as amazing and amusing. This is important not only for me, but for all those whom I infect and influence with my mood.

Through our own personal practices, we can change the way we respond to any phenomenon that comes our way. I use the word "phenomenon" simply to mean "what is." Everything that happens is a phenomenon. Our suffering begins when we attach a belief or a story to what happens. For example, *story* about phenomena might sound like this: "She was pissed off at the meeting this morning." The phenomena themselves are, "She did not speak at the meeting this morning. She was sitting with her arms crossed." When we adopt the personal practice of refusing to create negative stories around phenomena, we can also avoid some of the suffering that proceeds from our assumptions. *Monkey Business* offers a wealth of personal practices that can help us succeed in "caring for all."

How *Monkey Business* Came to Be

I was attending a World Laughter Tour Advanced Laughter Leader Workshop in Columbus, Ohio, in November 2005. Marilyn Sprague-Smith, MEd, CLL, closed our training with a workshop entitled "How to Gain a Fat PR Portfolio and Broaden Your Bottom Line." Marilyn is an award-winning consultant, professional speaker, author, and certified laughter leader. After she got us charged up with ideas, we each partnered with another participant to brainstorm about how we might put some of these ideas into action.

One way Marilyn mentioned to establish credibility and increase visibility was to get published. I told my partner, a lovely laughter leader from Kansas named Adrienne Edmondson, about my affiliation with Frisky's Wildlife and Primate Sanctuary. She excitedly offered the suggestion that I could write a column called "Life Is a Barrel of Monkeys." I loved the idea and played with it in my mind on the flight back to Maryland. It became clear to me how I could tie all of my current commitments and passions together. The idea for my new column, "Monkey Business—Better Business Practices Learned Through Monkeys," was born in the air somewhere between Columbus and Baltimore. I wrote three columns in the first week I was back and then one per month after that until I reached my fiftieth column.

After observing thousands of hours of human workplace behavior and hundreds of hours of monkey behavior, I noticed there was a connection. Each chapter in this book makes a connection between the monkey featured in the story and a human workplace situation.

The chapters in this book are grouped into six parts, with the chapters in each part all centered around a common theme. Individual chapters open with a short quotation to set the tone, introduce a monkey behavior observed during my volunteer work at Frisky's, and then offer a related human workplace behavior based in monkey wisdom. Throughout the chapters, I have included examples from authors who have given their blessing for their words to serve as springboards for points I am making.

As I began to consider how to bring all of my "Monkey Business" columns together in one book, the writing evolved yet again. The pieces that had begun as separate, standalone monthly columns now came together, and a common identity began to form. Many shared themes emerged from the individual pieces of writing—themes that reflect my values, my philosophy about life, and my journey with Tai Sophia, Science of Mind, and Frisky's Wildlife and Primate Sanctuary most especially. Those themes are reflected in the part titles for the book's table of contents: "Creating an Environment Where Possibility Thrives," "Acknowledging Our Shared Humanity," "Getting Along," "Communicating with Awareness," "Evolving Our Business Paradigm," and "Opening to Optimism." When I look at these part titles, I see a mirror for all of the beliefs that I do my best to embody in my daily life and choices.

As you read, you'll notice that some of the names recur from chapter to chapter. I did this deliberately, arranging the material so that you can read the chapters in any order. Feel free to skip around or read the whole book cover to cover, as you like. To help you remember who's who, you might want to refer to the "Cast of Characters" that I've included after the table of contents in the front of this book. It lists the name of each monkey who resides at Frisky's Wildlife and Primate Sanctuary, as well as the names of people who appear in this book more than once or who have had a major influence on me. To my readers who might be considered "perfectionists" or just really good at math, I added the thirty-eighth chapter after having the book cover designed. Instead of changing the title, I have kept it at "37 Better Business Practices" just because I like the way it sounds better than "38 Better Business Practices." Perhaps an example of staying open to possibility?

<u>Some Suggestions for How to Use This Book</u>

To tell you how to read this book seems a bit presumptuous on my part. However, I offer you my vision of how this book can be put to best use. Although the practices described in *Monkey Business* are straightforward, they are not necessarily simple. When we take responsibility for being the creators of our stories, our lives, and our experience, we are committing to an ongoing process that takes steadfast, mindful practice. Such practice is best done in small steps.

I envision you reading just one chapter a week, and practicing or meditating on the chapter's offering for that entire week. Observe how life shows up for you when you are looking at this possibility or using this practice. A chapter a week will help you retain this practice, making it easier to incorporate it fully into your life. Using the stories and suggestions included in each chapter as practices for daily living can help to reduce suffering and open your heart and mind to greater possibility.

For a deeper experience and a bigger commitment to practice, keep a daily journal of your thoughts and observations. Allowing yourself to write freely without stopping or editing is a powerful way both to access and activate the energies of the unconscious, nonlinear mind.

We use linear thinking, which is based on past experiences and what we already know, during our waking hours. Linear thinking is logical. Choose a starting point and then complete step one. Step two follows upon the completion of step one, and so on. In nonlinear thinking, there can be many starting points with the ideas springing off in all directions and at the same time. This is where breakthroughs occur. The tactile act of writing with pen on paper can help to take us into the deeper realms of our being. The physical act of the hand moving the pen across the page creates a meditative rhythm. Speech is linear, while thoughts when writing tend to be nonlinear. Through nonlinear thinking, we discover insights by curbing our mental reflex to think only in terms of what we know. Journaling is an effective way to connect with the deeper realms of self.

My Hopes for *Monkey Business*

I wrote this book to raise awareness of Frisky's Wildlife and Primate Sanctuary, a very special place that serves Howard County, Maryland, and beyond. A portion of the proceeds from every book sold will be donated to Frisky's.

It is our shared responsibility to care for this earth and the well-being of the creatures that inhabit it. We human beings are also animals, and we are all interconnected. Everything is linked. Nothing is self-sufficient. When our fellow creatures' well-being suffers, so does our own well-being as a species. Each species has a role to play, and it affects the roles of others. With every day that passes, we become more and more aware that biodiversity is *vital.* Our health, our food, and our existence literally depend on the well-being of all. I wanted not only to communicate that through this book, but to make a contribution toward greater well-being for all.

Ultimately, *Monkey Business—37 Better Business Practices Learned Through Monkeys* is a book about transformative leadership. It offers life practices for the workplace that, when done with compassion and commitment, can be life-changing. How we operate in the workplace will affect how we operate in our personal time, and vice versa. To me, separating how we behave in these two realms is like separating body from mind. Transformative leadership practices change the way we offer ourselves to our colleagues in the workplace, to our families, to our neighbors and friends, and to the world. When we change as individuals, the situations around us begin to change as well.

I see *life* as our workplace. Our life *is* our business, and we are the leaders of it.

Important Note

Please note that it is illegal to take a wild animal into captivity for any reason unless you have the proper licenses and permits to do so. This is to protect both you and the animal and to help prevent the spread of disease.

It is illegal in most states to keep a monkey as a pet. In the states that have not yet outlawed them as pets, permits are required from the state. Having a monkey in your home illegally will lead to confiscation, fines, and possible euthanization of the monkey. Please do not do this to the monkey or to yourself.

Part 1: Creating an Environment Where Possibility Thrives

My Space

If you have debt I'm willing to bet that general clutter is a problem for you too.

—Suze Orman (personal finance expert)

Creating an environment where possibility thrives sometimes calls for some housecleaning.

When I arrived at Frisky's Wildlife Sanctuary for my volunteer work on this particular day, I could see many things that needed to be done. So I took out a pen and a piece of paper and made a list—for me, that's a sure way to get things accomplished. Once something is on my list, I feel compelled to do it. I set about completing the tasks, feeling a great sense of accomplishment every time I checked an item off the list.

When it was almost time for me to leave, I knew I wouldn't feel satisfied if I hadn't completed the whole list. The last item remaining was to sweep the floor around all the animals' enclosures in the main house. This area houses both birds and monkeys, and they have at least one thing in common—they make huge messes! I started in on the task.

Bonnie, another volunteer, had just arrived, and to help me get the job done, she grabbed the dustpan and trash bin. This encouraged me to sweep faster. Bits of paper and seeds lay all around and under the enclosures, so I began moving cages out to get to everything that had fallen behind them. As I got to the cage of Oogie, a fifteen-year-old cinnamon capuchin monkey, I picked up the pace even more. Her enclosure is on wheels, and I grabbed both corners and started to push it out of the way.

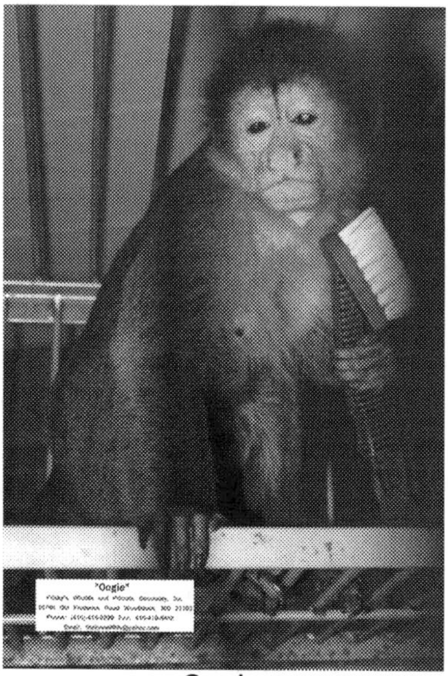

Oogie

Now, Oogie has diabetes and is blind in one eye, but that doesn't mean she's slow. To my complete surprise, she went ballistic. Oogie was like a firecracker shooting off in all directions, with a deafening *bang!* on the bars of the cage each time she hit the side. Her actions set off the other monkeys, who all started squealing—and then the birds joined in!

Long after Oogie had settled down, Sweetie, an umbrella cockatoo bird, was still squawking—and she kept it up for about ten minutes. By this time Colleen, the sanctuary manager, had come running in to see what all the fuss was about. Sweetie went on as if she were reciting everything to Colleen: "… and then she had the nerve to move my enclosure and sweep up everything I worked on for the past twelve hours … and then … "

"Tattletale," Bonnie said.

How similar is this to how we humans behave when someone comes in and messes with our "stuff"? Everyone knows at least one person at work—and maybe you are that person—who has piles of stuff on and around his or her desk. To a visitor, the piles might look like a huge, unorganized mess. But not to the one the desk belongs to. In fact, if asked to clean it up, the owner would probably say he couldn't part with a single piece of paper—and then give you a reason why. That person might even have a sign in his office that says, "If you don't like my mess, go away."

Feng shui expert Stephanie Roberts writes on her "Fast Feng Shui" website about the emotional aspects of clutter clearing:

> Getting rid of books and magazines we don't have time to read means accepting that we don't have enough time or attention to explore every topic that is of interest to us. If you lack confidence in pursuing a long-held dream, keeping your clutter can keep you from going out and doing it. If you grew up poor and hungry, surrounding yourself with material goods may feel reassuring that you will always have enough. Maybe the clutter makes you feel and look important and busy. You are busy—looking for things you can't find.

Don Aslett, in his book *The Office Clutter Cure,* cites many instances of people who have lost business because they made others wait too long for needed information. In one example, a person looking for something else found a five hundred dollar check that had *expired.* "What can a messy office desk cost you? Lost jobs, late or never completed assignments, alienated clients and customers, injuries, and maybe even a failed marriage." (p. 22)

Clean desks get promoted. They allow abundance into our lives in all sorts of ways. In *Keys to the Kingdom,* David Owen Ritz writes, "Physical objects are really spiritual energy. Energy must flow to do its work. When stagnation exists in any energy system, creation cannot take place. Conversely, when the flow of energy is free and abundant, the power to create is also abundant"

So, maybe Oogie wouldn't get a promotion—but she can teach us that the motivation to tidy up has to come from within rather than someone just forcing the organization and tidiness upon you.

Weekly Practice

> *Where in your own life can you make space for possibility? Is there mental or physical clutter that you need to clear? Declutter a closet, a desk, or a room.*

Selected Resources

Aslett, Don. *The Office Clutter Cure.* P. 22. Avon, MA: Adams Media, 2008.

Ritz, David Ritz. *The Keys to the Kingdom*. Workbook that accompanies the class CDs, 2002. www.newthoughtsforliving.com.

Roberts, Stephanie. "Feng Shui Articles." *Fast Feng Shui.* Accessed 21 September 2010.
http://www.fastfengshui.com/articles.htm#clutterseries.

Movement

Movement is a medicine for creating change in a person's physical, emotional, and mental states.

—Carol Welch

"All around the mulberry bush, the monkey chased the weasel..." Oogie, a 7.2 pound cinnamon capuchin monkey at Frisky's (also featured in chapter one), loves to hold my hands and bounce up and down to this song. Our interactions are rarely passive, as many human-to-human interactions are. For instance, there's never been a time when we've sat and had a cup of coffee together (or the monkey equivalent). A place like Starbucks would never go over well in a nonhuman primate society—and besides, I think monkeys are born with caffeine in their bloodstreams. For Oogie, our interactions are all about movement.

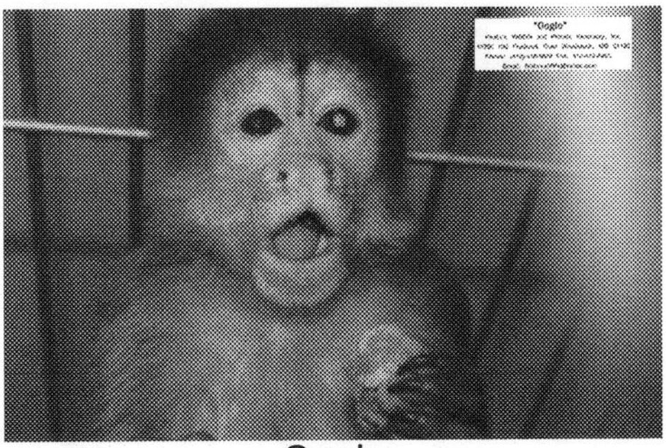

Oogie

Some humans have made the connection between physical movement and being more open to a new way of thinking about something. Take Lisa Morrel, a brilliant lifestyle coach, who has come up with a creative way to combine the two things she likes most in her business. Lisa has a passion for helping people realize their true potential and live with more joy, passion, and peace in their everyday experience. She also has a passion for fitness and wellness. Although Lisa loves lifestyle coaching, the traditional one-on-one conversation within the confines of four walls did not appeal to her. Lisa envisioned people opening up and talking while they walk. So she started offering a unique type of coaching session called *Walk and Talk.* This session combines personal lifestyle coaching with aerobic walking, allowing the client to achieve fitness goals during coaching sessions. Lisa travels to a location that is convenient for her client.

Someone else who has discovered the value of movement is author and Zen practitioner Andi Young. In her book, *The Sacred Art of Bowing: Preparing To Practice,* Young speaks to how we can change our perspective through movement. "As we change our posture, we become more mindful of our emotions. The moment we take to shift our bodies is also a moment to shift our perspective away from the mundane and toward the divine or exemplary".

Imagine what moving or shifting our bodies on a regular basis in the workplace could do for our productivity and creativity—not to mention our physical health. In Saskatchewan, Canada, some businesses have started doing just that.

Evidence shows that workplace wellness programs improve productivity, enhance job satisfaction, and reduce sick leave, absenteeism, job stress, and injuries. Saskatchewan's *in motion* workplace campaign is a province-wide movement that aims to increase people's physical activity at work for all of these reasons. An *in motion* workplace values the benefits of physical activity and creates a supportive environment for employees to become more physically active—all ways of creating an environment where possibility thrives. The campaign's official website, www.saskatchewaninmotion.ca, suggests activities that not only help people incorporate fitness practices at work, such as using human-powered modes of transportation to get to work (walking, cycling, skating), but that also make for a cleaner environment and improved health. Other ideas include taking walk breaks instead of coffee breaks, using the stairs instead of elevators, and keeping free weights and resistance bands in the break room. Could there be a more convenient and cost-saving environment in which to exercise than the workplace?

Oogie and I have another song we like to groove to:

> Ten little monkeys jumping on the bed.
> One fell off and bumped her head.
> Mama called the doctor and the doctor said,
> "No more monkeys jumping on the bed!"
> Come to think of it, all these monkey songs are about movement.

Thank you, Oogie—I think we're beginning to get it!

Weekly Practice

> *Take a pre-assessment of your physical and emotional state before you begin exercise or movement for any length of time. A good session of laughter exercises is also considered a mild form of exercise. You do not have to be in a "feel good" state of mind before you start, just willing. After the movement or exercise is complete, take a post-assessment of your emotional and physical state. Notice if your perspective has shifted in any way.*

Selected Resources

Morrel, Lisa. "Perspective on Health." *The Business Monthly.* Accessed 23 September 2010, http://209.116.252.254/1_2004_focus/f_22.html

Saskatchewan in motion. "What's an *in motion* workplace?" Accessed 23 September 2010, www.saskatchewaninmotion.ca.

Young, Andi. *The Sacred Art of Bowing: Preparing to Practice.* Woodstock, VT: SkyLight Paths Publishing, 2003.

Metaphors

The logic of the emotional mind is associative; it takes elements that symbolize a reality, or trigger a memory of it, to be the same as that reality. That is why similes, metaphors, and images speak directly to the emotional mind ... If the emotional mind follows this logic and its rules, with one element standing for another, things need not necessarily be defined by their objective identity: what matters is how they are perceived.

—Daniel Goleman, *Emotional Intelligence*

Willie puts his Monkey Chow Biscuits into a film canister and chews on the canister until the biscuit crumbles. He then dumps out the crumbs and eats them. You see, Willie, a wedge-capped capuchin monkey, has no canines. Rather than give up eating the biscuits, though, he got creative. The inventor of peanut butter probably acted on a similar inspiration. Although the product's actual history can't be verified, according to some accounts, its inventor was an unknown St. Louis physician who in 1890 encouraged the owner of a food products company to process and package ground peanut paste. He thought it would be a nutritious protein substitute for people with poor teeth who couldn't chew meat.

Willie isn't the only clever monkey at Frisky's. Isadora makes a hammock out of a sheet by weaving ends through the chain link fence so that she can lie in it. The capuchin monkeys will lasso a runaway grape with a sheet or a towel, if it has landed outside their enclosure. The Frisky's volunteers have seen both Kiko (a rhesus macaque) and Grisha (a Geoffrey marmoset), use a mirror to see around corners.

If you think about it, running out of something or not having the money to buy a desired item can be great fuel for creativity. When we have everything we need right at our fingertips, our mind has no need to stretch. It can become lazy. I don't know about you, but I would be hard pressed to figure out a mathematical problem using long division anymore. I panic if the calculator goes missing from the kitchen drawer.

So how can we encourage innovative possibilities like these to thrive in our own work environments? For one thing, when we want an out-of-the-ordinary result, we can put our thinking caps on and use the creative powers that are our birthright.

My father and I witnessed these powers in action on our annual father-daughter trip. This year, we went to see a couple of beautiful buildings in Washington, DC, that I had never been inside before. While touring the Folger Shakespeare Library, we were invited to step into the Shakespeare theater, which is designed to look like a theater from Elizabethan times. As we sat watching the middle school students who were there on a field trip, we were delighted to witness the creativity unfolding onstage from these young, brilliant minds. Students took turns walking across the stage holding an object, saying, in their best Shakespearean language, "'Tis not a ______; 'tis a ______." The one I remember most was "'Tis not a pencil; 'tis a drapery rod for a faerie." Imagine what might happen if you set up a stage and tried this one at work!

So what if you have every high-tech gadget you need to get your work done, yet you still feel stagnant? Following are some simple, yet brilliant examples that show how new ideas can unexpectedly take form.

Michael Cronan is the founder of an advertising agency in Berkeley, California, that has come up with the names of several hugely successful products. In 2009, *The San Francisco Chronicle* ran an article by Steve Rubenstein titled, "How Michael Cronan Spells Success."

> At the end of a winding street in the Berkeley hills is a bag of old Scrabble tiles that is changing the world.
>
> It's amazing how many important-sounding words can be made up by grabbing letters out of the bag and playing around with them. TiVo, for instance. When "tivo" came out of the bag 10 years ago, it didn't mean anything. Now TiVo means nothing less than the future of that great god, television.
>
> Michael Cronan made that word up, using his imagination and the Scrabble tiles. Cronan makes up words for a living. He also designs product brands to go with the made-up words. He's what's known in the design industry as a "brandparent."

Juanita Weaver, creativity consultant and coach, suggests using metaphors (comparing your situation to something else) to get creative ideas flowing. Let's say you want to increase sales and are having trouble coming up with good strategies. Using the metaphor technique, you might ask yourself how selling your product or service is like doing stand-up comedy or baking a cake. From Weaver's 2003 article in *Entrepreneur*:

> Here's how you can use this technique in your business. If you have a question or problem you're trying to solve, choose an object or an action. (Metaphors depicting an action are usually more evocative.)
>
> Going further, choose an activity you have some emotional reaction to, whether it's good or bad. If you have a hard time coming up with an idea, try one of the following examples: going on a diet, doing stand-up comedy, running for political office, riding a bike, running a day-care center, cooking a fancy meal or disciplining a child.

Think of as many characteristics of the action or object as possible. Then see what this sparks about your current situation. Use several metaphors to generate even more ideas. The constant generation of new ideas is a crucial element in business. Often, the simplest techniques can spark the most prolific flow of ideas.

When choosing an object or action for your own metaphor, remember, any activity will do—don't get hung up on trying to get the best metaphor. You'll be amazed how quickly you arrive at some innovative solutions.

The principals of Frisky's Creative Consulting Firm—Willie, CEO; Isadora, President; and Creative Partners Kiko and Grisha—are not available by phone or e-mail. But I'll keep you posted on their next creative venture.

Grisha

Isadora

"'tis not an apple ..."

Kiko

Willie

Weekly Practice

> *Both Cronan and Weaver encouraged their creativity to unfold by using familiar objects, words, or situations in new ways. How might you put your creativity to work in a similar way in your own work life?*

Selected Resources

Rubenstein, Steve. "How Michael Cronan Spells Success." *The San Francisco Chronicle*, 26 June 2009. Article accessed online July 2009.

Weaver, Juanita. "Mental Images: Using Metaphors Can Get A River of Creative Juices Flowing." *Entrepreneur* May 1, 2003. http://www.entrepreneur.com/article/61112.

Gardens and Grace

A light wind swept over the corn, and all nature laughed in the sunshine.

—Anne Bronte

The feeding of the guests and residents at Frisky's Sanctuary starts early. Before Colleen eats her own breakfast, she checks on all of those in her care, making sure their needs are met and they're all safe.

Recently, she entered the macaque monkey house and discovered CoCo, a twenty-two-year-old rhesus macaque with diabetes, on the floor with a black eye. Colleen immediately applied an antibiotic ointment to his eye, made sure he was able to sit up to eat and drink, and consulted with Dr. Keith Gold, a veterinarian at Chadwell Animal Hospital in Abingdon, Maryland, and Frisky's veterinary consultant.

CoCo

In order to keep the sunlight out of his irritated eye, Colleen locked CoCo's tunnel door, which gives him outdoor access. After two days of being indoors, we sensed he had a bad case of cabin fever, so we unlocked the tunnel door and let him go back out. Sunlight might be hard on an irritated eye, but it helps the body, whether monkey or human, produce a chemical that makes us feel happier. It also triggers the body to make its own vitamin D, a crucial nutrient with roles in building strong bones, healthy teeth, and in maintaining a strong immune system.

Sunlight and green spaces are so important that organizations have sprung up to educate people about them. One of these is the "Gardens and Grace Conference," which hosts gatherings in various locations. The 2008 conference was held in Baltimore, Maryland. Workshop speakers Tom Stoner and Carolyn Rapp gave presentations about the TKF Foundation, founded in 1996 by Tom and Kitty Stoner. The TKF Foundation's mission is to provide the opportunity for a deeper human experience by supporting the creation of public green spaces and gardens that offer a temporary place of sanctuary in troubled areas.

As Stoner and Rapp describe it in their book, *Open Spaces, Sacred Places*, "Over time, [the green spaces' makers] have created a distinct zone of safety, an understood division between the violence of the neighborhood and the peace within this sacred garden." (p. 36) These spaces encourage reflection, provide solace, and engender peace. Each garden has a beautiful bench to sit on and a cubby underneath the bench that holds a journal for recording the visitor's thoughts.

I had the privilege of visiting three such green spaces in the heart of Baltimore's most drug-affected neighborhoods. One is behind the Amazing Grace Lutheran Church in the McElderry Park community of East Baltimore. The pastor of the church, Karen Brau, took us to the gardens and labyrinth, called The Amazing Port Street Sacred Commons. It was created in 2001, following Karen's vision to create a haven in the midst of blight. The entire community is welcome to seek solace there. Karen's aim was to take back the neighborhood from the violence and the drug dealers, one step at a time.

As we entered this space, our attention was immediately drawn to a large butterfly bush loaded with monarch butterflies. While Karen and the rest of us squealed with delight, the butterflies lifted off the bush and circled above and around us, as if they were celebrating with us. It seemed that they danced to our joy. Never had Karen seen more than one or two at a time in the garden; that day, there might have been a hundred. Once we had quieted and began to walk the labyrinth, they settled back down into the bush. Never would I have imagined such beauty amid such ugliness. That day will be forever imprinted in my soul.

Another of the TKF-supported spaces, featured in Stoner and Rapp's book, is the Meditation Garden at the Western Correctional Institution in Cumberland, Maryland, home to more than 1,700 inmates and staff. The warden, Jon Galley, recognized that for the inmates, "there was no place to take a moment to experience just a sliver of humanity." He realized that many of the prisoners under his care would one day return home, and he wanted to offer them an opportunity to heal and learn before they were released.

So the prisoners and Wayne Yoder, a local biology professor, spent countless hours tilling the land and planting. The prisoners were invested in this project—they, along with architect Tony Lawlor, had decided what they wanted in it and helped design it. (Stoner and Rapp, p. 95) One of the prisoners said, "Today, I became someone different. I made something very special come alive. A place was built where we could sit, think, get outside, and get our minds together".

In architect Tony Lawlor's words:

> One of the inmates said to me, "I've done a lot of destructive things in my life. Making this garden is a chance for me to do something positive." I think that's why they take such good care of the garden. It's a place that honors their humanity in an environment where they have to put on their emotional armor to survive.

I think that we can sometimes feel like prisoners of our jobs. We create our own mental prisons with our inflexible or self-defeating beliefs. What if your workplace had a garden or green space where you were free to go whenever you needed to look at a challenge in a fresh light? Vegetable gardens at work are another possibility for creating community and healing. A row or two could even be planted for the homeless. Soup kitchens are always in need of fresh vegetables. Gardens and nature let us recharge our souls and open up our thoughts and our spirits to possibility.

CoCo has never read the book *Open Spaces, Sacred Places,* nor did he attend the conference. It is just anchored in his awareness that nature is a healer. It wraps its loving arms around us and holds us until we feel better.

Weekly Practice

> *Spend fifteen minutes each day this week out in nature. Sit or walk in a garden, yard, or park. Observe any shifts in your body or your thoughts.*

Selected Resources

"Care for the Earth, Care for the City, Care for the Soul: Gardens and Grace III, Baltimore." *Gardens and Grace.* Accessed 24 September 2010. www.ang-md.org/gardensandgrace/.

Stoner, Tom, and Carolyn Rapp. *Open Spaces, Sacred Places.* P. 95, Annapolis, MD: TKF Foundation, 2008.

Guilty

Guilt is regret for what we've done. Regret is guilt for what we didn't do.

—Anonymous

A woman at a Weight Watchers meeting spends the first five minutes berating herself because two nights ago she sat down and ate an entire chocolate cake. After five minutes of this, the group facilitator stops her by saying, "Enough! Just call it a carrot and get over it!"

Is it possible that guilt is a contributing factor to what puts the weight on? Whatever the case, it certainly closes our minds and hearts to greater possibility.

Speaking of cake, I've often noticed that Bonnie, a member of the board of directors at Frisky's, never misses a monkey's birthday. Every month, she brings miniature cupcakes and offers all the monkeys a sweet treat to celebrate the ones who have birthdays that month. All the monkeys eagerly take a cupcake. Not

Kiko

one of them pauses to wonder whether they "should" or "should not" eat one. Some of them even try reaching for a second or third. Kiko, a twelve-year-old male rhesus macaque, would take the entire tray if given the chance—and show no signs of guilt or regret the next morning. Kiko likes the way he looks. He proudly pats his "buns of steel" for everyone to admire.

We humans tend to take the often untrue "noise" in our heads, like the voice that says, "I should," for gospel. That kind of guilt is what keeps us staying late each night at the office, and also what has us bringing work home over the weekend. For some of us, the noise is so loud that we even skip vacation. We don't want anyone to think that *we* might not be carrying our share of the workload by leaving earlier than they do! In fact, the others may be staying late because *they* feel guilty about leaving before we do.

Early in life, I learned that if I had permission to do something, I could do it guilt-free. I have carried that into adulthood. Receiving permission seems to lift a load off my shoulders. Reflecting on her childhood, Rita Dove, US poet laureate from 1993 to 1995, captures the feeling of freedom that permission brings: "Going to the library was the one place we got to go without asking for permission. And they let us choose what we wanted to read. It was a feeling of having a book be mine in its entirety." What she received was *permission* not to have to ask permission.

Wynonna Judd is another public figure who has learned to give herself permission: "I've learned lately that no one is going to hand me a permission slip and tell me to take time out for me." Good for you, Wynonna!

Perhaps a new practice in our own lives might be to give permission to people when we suspect that's the support they need to free themselves from their own mental prison of guilt. For example, if you hear someone at work saying something like, "I really should stay late tonight and finish up this report," try saying, "I give you permission to leave at five p.m. tonight." Give them a permission slip and free them from their prison.

Kiko proudly pats his "buns"—he is free from guilt. He does not have the noise in his head that says "I should" or "I shouldn't." Perhaps we would do well to take a lesson from him. When we quiet that noise in our own heads, it makes room for the voice of new possibilities.

Weekly Practice

Notice when the words "I should" come across your lips or even into your consciousness. Ask yourself if this is a self-created emergency or imprisonment. Is it true that you "should" or "shouldn't"? How does it feel if you use the words "I choose to" or "I choose not to" in place of "should" or "shouldn't"? Being aware of your negative or guilty thoughts helps you to manage the negative thoughts better. Awareness is transformational.

Alternate Role

And the day came when the risk to remain tight in a bud
was more painful than the risk it took to blossom.

—Anais Nin

Patsy would be leaving us very soon. It had become obvious that the leukemia had taken over and her body was giving in. We had tried everything we knew to prolong her life and keep her comfortable. Her mate, Gizmo, had even given his blood for a transfusion for Patsy. She lived for six months after it. We called Gizmo "our hero."

Patsy and Gizmo, both rhesus macaques, had shared an enclosure for fourteen years. They knew each other well, as long-time mates so often do. They had the comfort of each other's presence, knowing that the other was there through the sad times, the joyful times, the quiet times, and the times of unknowing. Gizmo has a quiet, gentle, passive way of being, while Patsy was always more aggressive. That is, until she got sick. Then the roles reversed.

In her own role as caregiver and Frisky's director, Colleen did not want to give up. She made every effort to ensure that Patsy was comfortable right until the very end. When Patsy stopped eating and drinking, we knew that her time was near. Colleen was frazzled and distraught, wondering if there was just one more thing that she could do. During the final forty-eight hours of Patsy's life, Colleen checked on her every hour. She felt some relief when Patsy lifted her head up off the blanket to look Colleen in the eyes, for what Colleen did not know at that moment was the last time.

One hour later, Gizmo would not let Colleen into the enclosure. His aggressive stance let Colleen know that she needed to leave them be. His tone told her, "I will take it from here—just leave her alone. There is nothing more to be done." For the sake of his Patsy, Gizmo took on the role of the aggressor. Within an hour of that interaction, Patsy's spirit left her body.

Patsy

We often take on an alternate role when a life situation calls for it. If a parent becomes incapacitated, we may take on the alternate role of caregiver. After losing a spouse, we take on the role of being single. If your company is about to make a big presentation to a client and your team leader becomes ill or has a family emergency, you take on the role of presenter. If you are the cook at a diner and the server doesn't show up, you take on the role of server. For the most part, these are unplanned situations in which we need to act without a lot of forethought. However, in certain life situations, we can and maybe *need* to take on an alternate role on purpose, in order to reach a goal or overcome an obstacle. We can prepare for these roles in advance.

One of our final class assignments at the Tai Sophia Institute was to play an alternate role—something completely different from our normal way of being, the role we were most comfortable playing. The intent of this exercise was to help us develop the ability to be flexible in our life roles—to take on any physical mode of being that is essential to be of service to the community. The assumption underlying the exercise is that the posture, tone of voice, and presence that we consider normal for us is "normal" only because we're so familiar with it that we take it for granted. We say "this is me" only because it's the "me" we have practiced. Our assignment challenged this assumption:

> Identify a quality you say you are not practiced in—for example, commanding, outrageous, flamboyant, sensual, shy, greedy, proper, businesslike. Then identify a well-known movie role or character that embodies this quality. Get the movie, identify a 30-second segment in which the character strongly embodies this quality, watch the segment several times, and practice mimicking the segment until you have a new embodiment. *Tip:* The quality and the role you choose must be a big stretch for you (Tai Sophia's alternate role assignment).

Our classmates helped each of us choose the role that we were to embody and act out in class. We knew they'd chosen the right one when we wanted to shout, "Oh no—*anything* but that!"

My classmates assigned me the role of Gordon Gekko, a greedy and heartless businessman played by Michael Douglas in the 1987 movie *Wall Street*. Gekko took what he wanted, regardless of who got hurt while he was getting it. I rented and watched the entire movie, finally choosing a scene in which Gekko was lecturing Bud Fox, played by Charlie Sheen, about how you can't care too much about "the other guy." Gekko saw money as a game. In order for him to win, somebody else had to lose.

To play this role, I had to take on Gekko's tone, his body stance, and his attitude. I thought I had it down after practicing this role for the entire week before I had to perform it. But my teacher, Dianne Connelly, was not convinced. She honed in on one line and had me say it again and again until my tone, my body, and my heartless glare matched the words. After about the fifth or six time, I felt myself *become* Gordon Gekko. Dianne felt it, too. She smiled and nodded.

I wasn't sure at the time just how playing the role of Gordon Gekko would serve me or anyone else. Aside from my role as volunteer director of community outreach at Frisky's, I have a speaking and teaching business in which I give workshops on therapeutic laughter. I'm trained as a Certified Laughter Leader, and I lead trainings for the World Laughter Tour. I also attend professional development conferences, keep up to date on research about the health benefits of laughter, and belong to associations that discuss the benefits of humor and laughter. I've invested in the equipment needed to put on a presentation and run a business. And yet I lacked the confidence to charge a fee high enough to cover my expenses and have a little money left over at the end of the day.

Thanks to the alternate-role exercise, I now take on some of the business-savvy qualities of Gekko. When stating my fee to a client, I take on Gekko's confidence, his stance, his knowledge of his value. If I can't cover my expenses, I can no longer offer my gift of therapeutic laughter. Through embodying Gordon Gekko, I've learned to take care of *me.* If I'm not taken care of, I can't take care of others.

I believe Gizmo and Patsy had a wordless agreement about how they wanted to share the final moments of Patsy's life. Gizmo took on the alternate role of aggressor so that we would understand this, too. It might have been a stretch for him, but he did it in service to his life mate, Patsy.

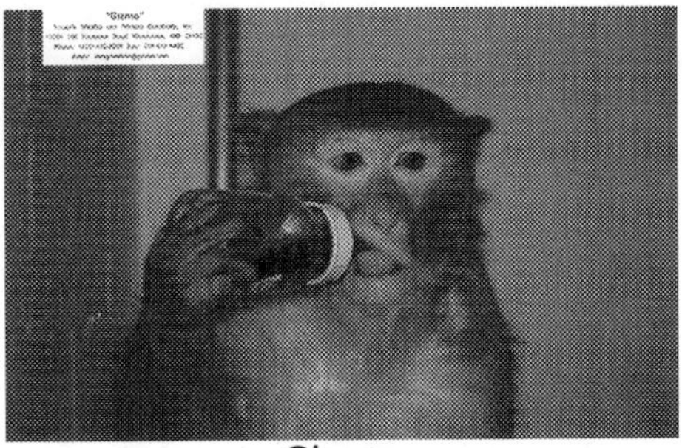

Gizmo

What alternate work role feels like the biggest stretch for you? I invite you to spend time practicing it. Then when the time comes that you need it, you'll be ready to play the new role that serves you and your colleagues best. And remember, if the stretch feels uncomfortable, that's what makes the room within you for all those new possibilities to thrive.

Weekly Practice

Identify an alternate role that is a stretch for you. Practice the embodiment of it as described in the exercise in this chapter. Note how taking on this role can serve you and/or others.

Part 2: Acknowledging Our Shared Humanity

Hugs

I will never forget our Free Hugs Campaign. A couple of people left their cars running and ran across the street to receive a hug from someone they had never met before. One woman thanked us and said we saved her from jumping off a bridge today.

—Heather Wandell

About a dozen committed volunteers were gathered in the makeshift recovery room (aka Colleen and Scott's bedroom/dining room/living room) at Frisky's the evening of the 2007 annual primate physicals. Dr. Keith Gold of Chadwell Animal Hospital and Dr. Michael Cranfield of the Maryland Zoo in Baltimore were preparing to anesthetize and do a complete physical on twenty-two monkeys that evening. The recovery room volunteers were excited about doing their part, which was to hold the monkeys (without bars to separate us) until the anesthesia began to wear off.

Gizmo and Me

While we were waiting for the first monkey to arrive in the recovery room from the infirmary, someone asked, "Who has a favorite that they definitely want to hold?"

"Gizmo!" I said. Gizmo, a thirty-two-pound rhesus macaque, was the first primate to come to Frisky's in 1989.

In the weeks after he'd lost his beloved Patsy, a female macaque, to leukemia, I had paid Gizmo lots of extra attention. I talked to him, read to him, and had the privilege of being in his enclosure with him. But never before had I held him or hugged him. To me, a hug is similar to bowing with hands in prayer position and saying, "Namaste." A hug also helps me to embody the same feeling: "The divinity in me honors the divinity in you." A hug honors our shared time on this earth together.

As I think back to the first time I participated in the primate physicals, I remember feeling disappointed that my favorite monkey at that time had already been held. Instead, I was handed Rachelle, a rhesus macaque whom I didn't know so well at the time. As Rachelle was very slow to come out of her anesthesia induced sleep, she and I spent an hour and a half in physical closeness that night before her insensibility began to wear off. In that short time, something changed. I felt a sense of *oneness* with her for the first time. After that night I continued to experience that feeling, and I still feel it each time I walk by what was once her enclosure, even though Rachelle has since made her transition to the nonphysical realm (death, as many would word it). I have embodied that knowing of oneness with her for life. All it took was a hug.

But is hugging appropriate with our coworkers and others with whom we do business?

Patricia Matthews, founder of Workplace Solutions Consultants, a St. Louis-based consulting company says, "I think hugging in the workplace depends a lot on the culture of that specific workplace. It's truly a gray area. Some people love to be hugged. For others it's 'please don't touch me.'" She added that organizations in recent years have been doing a better job of bringing in employees that fit their culture—whether it's pro- or antihug.

A couple of years ago, I was one of several members in attendance at a meeting of the Coalition of Geriatric Services (COGS) programs committee. Although my memory fails me around the conversation that was going on as we stood up to leave the meeting, I do clearly remember one gentleman on the committee saying, "You know, it's not all about being huggy-kissy."

I remember finding it hard to hold back a giggle. As a matter of fact, I didn't hold it back at all—I said, "It isn't? I thought that *is* what it's all about. Come on, give me a hug!" So he smiled and we hugged. The mood lightened and several hugs were shared among all who were present. Another option would have been to have left the meeting feeling frustrated over the situation he had commented on.

It feels much better to me to hug someone I have known for some time at a business or networking meeting than it does to extend a hand for a formal handshake. We don't have to be best friends or agree with another person's business ethics to acknowledge that we are one with them. We are not separate—that is an illusion. For me, a hug is the most genuine way I know to acknowledge another's presence and our connectedness. With some people, however, it is clear that a handshake will suffice.

In an article by Mark Sheffert, titled "Hug Your Way To Success," Sheffert describes the story of a man named Jack Mitchell. Mitchell is the CEO of Mitchells/Richards, a high-end men's clothing retailer in Connecticut and New York that outfits the Fortune 500 executives who work on Wall Street. Mitchell had come to Sheffert's home town for a speaking engagement about his books *Hug Your Customers: The Proven Way to Personalize Sales and Achieve Astounding Results* and *Hug Your People: The Proven Way to Hire, Inspire, and Recognize Your Employees and Achieve Remarkable Results.* Sheffert relays the story of how Mitchell's parents founded the apparel chain in 1958 with only three suits, a couple dozen shirts, some socks, and a handful of ties. Today, the Mitchells sell $65 million annually in apparel. Naturally, the inventory has grown quite a bit from the early days. But it's much more than just the inventory that keeps the customers coming back. Mitchell says it's the *relationships* the family builds with the customers. Mitchell says that his parents understood that there were things that the customer wanted more than the inventory or even a great location— they include a friendly greeting, a personal interest in the customer, a shop that makes them feel special, and a "no-problem" attitude. The company still runs on the founders values today.

In an interview after the talk, Sheffert asked Mitchell if he really hugs all of his customers. Mitchell replied:

> "Absolutely!" Being a bright guy, he picked up on the doubt that was showing in [Sheffert's] expression. He explained that hugging doesn't have to mean wrapping his arms around everyone who walks in the door. It means doing things for his customers that go beyond what they expect of a retailer. He says it's about building a personal relationship with every transaction, because "that's what people want."

I truly believe Rachelle was out for so long from the anesthesia that night so that I could have a chance to not just build a relationship with her, but experience an embodied sense of oneness. The lived experience of it is completely different from just reading about it.

So why not invite that experience into your workplace today? You might start by putting a sign on your desk that says "Free Hugs." Rather than approach people to offer them a hug, let them come to you. It's a wonderful chance for all of us to acknowledge each other's presence in a simple but profound way that gives us a felt sense of our oneness. Go on, take a risk! We're all in this together, doing the best we can between breakfast and bedtime.

Weekly Practice

> *What opportunities can you create in your own workplace to "lift someone up"? If not a "free hugs" sign, could it be a "free laughs" sign or "free smiles" sign? Are you observing the reactions or judging the reactions?*

Selected Resources

Matthew, Patricia quote from an online article by Ruth Mantell, "To Hug or Not To Hug." Accessed online 2/19/12, MarketWatch, September 21, 2007, at http://finance.yahoo.com/news/pf_article_103549.html

Sheffert, Mark, "Hug Your Way To Success." Twin Cities Business. August 2008. Article accessed online 2/21/12 at http://www.tcbmag.com/ideasopinions/corneroffice/104192p1.aspx

Impermanence

Oh, this is the joy of the rose:
That it blows,
And goes.

—Willa Cather

A friend of mine since childhood, Mark, e-mailed me an article titled "Caring for Senior Zoo Citizens Getting Trickier." The article describes how many different zoos around the country are facing the challenges of caring for elderly animals such as Rollie, an emperor tamarin monkey who lives at the Lincoln Park Zoo in Chicago. Rollie is seventeen years old, an age that he almost certainly never would have reached if he had remained in his natural Amazon habitat. At the time the article was written, he had only six teeth left out of 32. Monkeys like Rollie rely on their teeth to help them crunch on raw vegetables, such as sweet potato.

The article mentioned another example from Texas. "At the El Paso Zoo, keepers noticed six years ago that Sheba, their regal black jaguar, was faltering. Worsening arthritis made it difficult for her to climb. Her kidneys were failing. Cataracts limited her ability to see." The zookeepers had recently made the difficult decision to administer euthanasia to Sheba, shutting her body down for good. Sheba was twenty-seven years old. The average lifespan of a jaguar in its natural habitat is twelve to sixteen years.

Rollie and Sheba are examples of how animals in captivity tend to live much longer than they do in their natural environments. Living in captivity grants them an exception to nature's survival laws.

Zoey

The staff at Frisky's faces the same challenges as the zookeepers in the article. For example, we recently had to make the difficult decision not to prolong the suffering for our little fourteen-year-old female Bolivian squirrel monkey, Zoey, whose weight had dropped to just half a pound. The average weight for one of her kind is one and a half to two pounds. She had been suffering for so many years with Crohn's disease that she no longer had any good days. It was a heartbreaking decision to have to make. Zoey was still so sweet-tempered, yet she seemed to be getting tinier every day. The ride to the vet's office was a tough one for volunteers Matt and Joyce Dietsch, who accompanied Zoey. It didn't help that I was standing there sobbing as she was being placed into the kennel cab for safe travel.

In Buddhism, one of the central beliefs is based on the *doctrine of impermanence*. This doctrine states that every conditioned existence, without exception, is inconstant and is always in flux. Life embodies this flux in the birth process, the aging process, and in the experience of loss. Thich Nhat Hanh, one of the world's most respected Zen masters, says:

> Nothing remains the same for two consecutive moments. Without impermanence, life is not possible. How can our daughter grow up into a beautiful young lady? How can we transform our suffering? How can the situation in the world improve? We need impermanence for social justice and hope.

Every day, there are new little ones arriving at Frisky's who need our help for a second chance at life. They remind us that our love is not all used up after we lose a loved one. They give us renewed hope, lift our spirits, and give us something to focus our energies on so that time can heal us.

Impermanence is ever-present in the workplace as well. An online article I read, "11 Ways to Fix Your Workplace Depression," reminded me that stress is impermanent, and so are deadlines. What might be a huge stress today at work will be completely different a month from now, and maybe even an hour from now. The article advises, "The next time you feel depressed or stressed at work, take a deep breath and say to yourself, 'This feeling will not last forever.'" Feelings are impermanent.

Our loss of Zoey woke me up to the impermanence of life. I remember her little squeal that sounded so much like a bird chirp. When I'd glance in her direction, she'd usually be leaning against the side of her enclosure so that I could come over and rub her back. How I miss that now. One of my teachers, Reverend Nancy Stepp of the Center for Spiritual Living—Laurel (Laurel, MD), reminded her congregation in one of her talks, "Everybody in our lives is only on loan to us."

Now that you have been reminded of that, will you talk to or treat someone differently today?

Weekly Practice

> *Impermanence is the constant, universal truth of change. Sights, sounds, smells, situations, and thoughts are constantly changing.*
>
> *Open the door or look out the window for a minute or two. Has everything remained exactly the same for that space of time? Do this every day this week. When you are at work and feeling upset about a situation, use this exercise as a reminder that life is in constant motion. The less we grasp and cling to any situation, the more ease there will be in the mind.*

Selected Resources

Associated Press. "Caring for Senior Zoo Citizens Getting Trickier." *MSNBC.com*. Accessed online 2/19/12. www.msnbc.msn.com/id/25265173.

Daily Mind, The. "11 Ways to Fix Your Workplace Depression." Accessed online 2/19/12. http://www.thedailymind.com/how-to/11-ways-to-fix-your-workplace-depression/.

Hanh, Thich Nhat. "The Three Dharma Seals." *A Buddhist Library*. Accessed online 11/21/11. http://www.abuddhistlibrary.com/Buddhism/G%20-%20TNH/TNH/The%20Three%20Dharma%20Seals/The%20Three%20Dharma%20Seals.htm

Inquiring Mind. "The Practice of Impermanence: An Interview with Joseph Goldstein." *Insight Meditation Society*. Accessed online 10/17/11. http://www.dharma.org/ims/joseph_goldstein_interview1.html

Feeling Important

Sometimes it is necessary to reteach a thing its loveliness.

—Galway Kinnell

I can hear Sandra Bullock now, in a sing-song voice, teasing her FBI-partner-turned-romantic-interest in the movie *Miss Congeniality.* Angel, a ten-pound mona guenon monkey at Frisky's, is doing her best Sandra Bullock imitation from the aforementioned scene.

Angel

"You think I'm *gorrrrr*-geous I know you *looooove* me I'm so im-*porrrrr*-tant." Angel's moves are so in sync with this little chant and her facial expression is so coy that you know she's just eating up your attention.

In the business world, a customer who receives attention from you is likely to remain a customer. Sandra Hicks, an independent consultant for the Swiss skin care and wellness company Arbonne International, makes it a regular practice to imagine that each person she interacts with is wearing a sign around their neck that says, "Make me feel important." And Sandra does just that—it's not luck that she's reached the rank of regional vice president. The world is a nicer place after an interaction with Sandra, thanks to the way she acknowledges each person's presence with such genuine attention.

Another example is executive chef Michael Miller of Harvard University's dining services. He tells how he went the extra mile to make sure one student was pleased with the university's food selections:

> I meet with the students in each house twice a year and I try to eliminate any bias I might bring with me from years of doing food service. I have to remember to listen to the students as my customers and provide service. One time a student said he missed his favorite soft drink, Minute Maid Orange Soda. I knew we couldn't physically fit another flavor into our machines and the standard response would have been to say, "I'm sorry, we can't accommodate you." But I decided he had the right to want his favorite soft drink, so I had the staff order two cases of it and send it to his room. It cost us less than $10 and he was thrilled. That's the kind of out of the box thinking we have to remember to do to be successful. Plus, it makes you feel good when you can solve a problem like that. (Yerkes, p. 33)

We may never fully understand why most people (and monkeys, too) need so much attention. Angel's story is unusual. Instead of her mother rejecting her (which occasionally happens), she rejected her mother. She would not let her mother feed or hold her, causing the mother emotional distress and baby Angel a near-death experience. Today, Angel still does not like to be touched, but she loves attention from her human friends, and it makes us feel good to give it. Better yet, we feel happy that she's allowing herself to receive it.

To receive with grace
May be the greatest giving.
There's no way I can separate the two.
When you give to me

I give to you my receiving.
When you take from me, I feel so given to.

—Ruth Bebermeyer, "Given To"

Notice where you might need the most practice—is it in the giving of attention or in the receiving of attention? Angel and her mother are reminders of what could happen emotionally to someone if you are not allowing yourself to receive.

Weekly Practice

> *Using Sandra's practice mentioned in this chapter, imagine everyone you interact with today is wearing a sign around their neck that says, "Make me feel important." How has this influenced your interactions?*

Selected Resources

Bebermeyer, Ruth. "Given To," from the album *Given To.* 1978.

Hicks, Sandra. Personal communication (approximate date—Fall 2004).

Yerkes, Leslie. *Fun Works: Creating Places Where People Love to Work.* San Francisco: Berrett-Koehler, 2007.

Presence

Lost yesterday, somewhere between sunrise and sunset,
two golden hours, each set with sixty diamond minutes.
No reward is offered for they are gone forever.

—Horace Mann

What would you think if someone you thought you had a great relationship with pulled up his lower lip, stuck up his nose, threw back his head, and walked away when you stopped to talk to him? It doesn't take hours of human psychology classes to know that a greeting like that isn't a warm one. That's exactly the kind of reception I'd been getting from Gizmo, a thirty-two-pound rhesus macaque, for several weeks in a row.

For some reason, I was now on Gizmo's *#%! list. Why me? I knew I hadn't been ignoring him—after all, I spoke his name just about every time I went by him on the way to the rabbit pens. One of my duties at the sanctuary is to get the domestic rabbits out for some exercise while I clean their enclosures and replenish their food and … ahhhh, wait a minute. Maybe it was the "went by him" part that Gizmo was upset about. *He* was never the one I was taking the time for, and he knew it. In a relationship, it means little to "whisper sweet nothings" to someone only in passing while never taking the time to truly be with them. It's our full presence and attention that lets others know they matter.

Ready to win back Gizmo's heart, I grabbed a lovely book from the Frisky's bookshelf that tells the life story of Saint Francis of Assisi, the patron saint of wildlife. The book's short chapters and colorful pictures made it a perfect choice for spending ten minutes here and there reading a couple of chapters aloud to Gizmo. It didn't take long for Gizmo to realize that now I was here to spend some time with *him*. As I read, he sat or lay down next to me. I have never gotten the "nose in the air/head toss" treatment again since we started our story time together. To save our relationship, I chose to put work aside momentarily. To this day, I believe it matters to him—and I know it matters to me.

Me reading to Gizmo

Our authentic presence with others communicates their value to us in a way that nothing else can. A story from Dr. Clifford C. Kuhn, aka "the Laugh Doctor," provides a poignant illustration of this truth.

Dr. Kuhn, a psychiatrist, medical school professor, and professional speaker, tells about the time he was invited to give the keynote address for the annual meeting of a national corporation. An audience of two hundred managers and supervisors applauded as the corporation's CEO stood before them to introduce Dr. Kuhn. In his introduction, the CEO lauded Dr. Kuhn's work with humor and gave his personal endorsement to the idea of having more fun in the corporate setting.

When Dr. Kuhn stepped up to the podium, the CEO shook his hand—then promptly left the room and did not return. As he disappeared from sight, so did the enthusiasm of the audience. The drop in energy was palpable. The CEO might as well have spoken the words, "Now, if you'll excuse me, you're not important enough for me to join you in having fun," because that's the message everyone received. Fun was had that morning, because you can't help but have fun in the presence of Dr. Kuhn, but nothing could restore the level of enthusiasm that was sucked out of the room when the CEO left it. (p. 124–125)

Presence is more than just making an appearance or going through the motions. It's being fully, authentically engaged with the one in front of us. Presence also goes much deeper than words alone. The CEO's unspoken communication with Dr. Kuhn came through loud and clear, much more so than the words of introduction he actually spoke.

Are you giving your full attention to the people you're with? Gizmo recognized when I wasn't giving him my full attention. So, being fellow primates, I would imagine your colleagues will also recognize if you are fully present, or if you're just "whispering sweet nothings" while passing through. When you, as a leader, commit to being fully present, it strengthens your team's willingness to commit to the same.

Weekly Practice

> *Be aware of being present in your interactions this week. Are you able to distinguish that difference between being present and not being present? Practice being with a coworker or family member for twenty minutes and not answering your phone or sending texts. Leave the phone out of hearing range if possible or turn it off completely for those twenty minutes. Notice how it feels. If you are anxious with this practice, then continue the practice until you notice ease in your mind and body.*

Selected Resources

Kuhn, Clifford C. *The Fun Factor.* P. 124—125. Louisville, KY: Minerva Books, 2003.

Excessive Celebration

There's a party goin' on right here
A celebration to last throughout the years
So bring your good times, and your laughter too
We gonna celebrate your party with you

—Kool & the Gang, from the song "Celebrate Good Times"

Willie squeals with delight, drools, puts out his hands, and nearly falls over with delirious celebration whenever I show up for a visit with him. It's not like it's been years since he's seen me—I'm there every week. Willie is an almost-ten-pound, wedge-capped capuchin monkey who came to Frisky's in February 1995, when his owner in San Diego developed a brain tumor and could no longer give Willie the care and attention that monkeys require. Some might label Willie's response to our time together "excessive celebration." Whatever others might think, I enjoy it.

Willie

The phrase "excessive celebration" brings to mind a high school football game of my son's that I attended in 2007. His team was the Vikings, and it was their ninth game of the season. The Mt. Hebron Vikings had a 0-8 record, and things weren't looking good for this game, either. The score was 21-0, with their opponent, Atholton, in the lead.

Vikings special teams member, Cesar Perez (#73), who had spent most of the season on the sidelines, was put into the game to join the punt return team. When the Vikings Richard Ireland (#89) blocked the punt made by Atholton, Cesar picked up the ball and ran with it for forty yards, scoring a touchdown.

Everyone went wild! The team ran onto the field, jumping for joy, and basically "dog-piling" Cesar. Everybody was cheering, jumping up and down, and hollering; players, fans, cheerleaders, and band members alike were having a jubilee.

And then we got smacked with a penalty—for "excessive celebration."

Even though we knew it was against the rules to celebrate publicly to this extent, the delight we felt over Cesar's success was irrepressible. In that moment, we were filled with the sheer joy of being alive. No how, no way could it be contained. We took the penalty with grace. After the game, my son Brad (#45) said, "This is something Cesar will be proud to share with his grandchildren."

This game was our own personal version of the movie *Invictus*. The 2009 film tells the true story of how the South African rugby team, the Springboks, won rugby's World Cup in 1995, the year when the team's native South Africa hosted the games. Morgan Freeman brilliantly played the role of Nelson Mandela, and Matt Damon played the role of François Pienaar, the captain of the South African team. The movie takes its name from the poem by English poet William Ernest Henley that kept Mandela inspired while serving a twenty-seven-year prison sentence. Mandela's and Pienaar's partnership inspired the rugby team to win that World Cup, and the movie's portrayal of it demonstrates the importance of shared celebration in building community, reuniting people, and finding common ground in a nation long divided by apartheid.

Writing about celebration, English clergyman Sydney Smith says, "The thing about performance, even if it is only an illusion, is that it is a celebration of the fact that we do contain within ourselves infinite possibilities." Thomas J. Peters writes, "Celebrate what you want to see more of."

The Vikings' community celebrated and cheered all over again at the annual football banquet as we watched the highlights from the 2007 season. We celebrated Cesar, and it was good!

The importance of celebration is gaining increasing attention. A book by corporate consultants Terrence Deal and M. M. Key, *Corporate Celebration: Play, Purpose, and Profit at Work,* reminds us of the value of celebration as a vehicle for creating bonding between individuals and community. Deal and Key write, "Celebrations infuse life with passion and purpose. They summon the human purpose. They attach us to our human roots and help us soar toward new visions. They touch our hearts and fire our imaginations. They bond people together and connect us to shared values and myths." (p. 5) Could celebrating even the "small" successes at work be a tool for increasing productivity?

Another example of celebration comes from the gthankyou.com blog. In a July 2008 blogpost, the writer talks about a company he used to work for, where the employees would gather after they received their paychecks and play "liar's poker" with the serial numbers on their checks. It always brought laughter. The writer speaks to what he learned from that job experience:

> About 10 years later I founded a venture-capital funded, technology-driven start-up company. Our team, mostly engineers, was talented and could work anywhere they wanted. The only reason they worked for my company is because they wanted to. Every payday I made a point of personally handing paychecks to *every* employee, looking them in the eye, using their names, and saying 'thank you'. Everyone knew the ritual. Every payday was a small celebration of thanks to each other for the continuing progress of a small, struggling company.

I once read that the reason people leave their car windows cracked in the parking lot when they go to work is that they have to leave most of who they are in the car, and they don't want it to suffocate. I have a feeling that's not a problem at the Scooter Store, Inc., a one-thousand-employee power wheelchair and scooter firm in New Braunfels, Texas. The company has a staff "celebrations assistant" whose job it is to throw confetti—twenty-five pounds a week—at employees. Excessive? Maybe, maybe not. Willie would be all over that!

The word "excessive" carries negative connotations. But "excessive" is a *human* judgment. Is our dog being excessive when she joyously greets us at the door, even though we've only been gone for a couple of hours?

Be excessive in celebrating. You can do it with or without gifts. In *Yes! Magazine,* Colin Beavan writes about the best and most meaningful Christmas he ever celebrated—with no material gifts exchanged. I don't know if I'm there yet, but Willie is. I don't need to give him a gift. My presence with him in the moment acknowledges his importance to me, and that's gift enough for him. It's enough of a celebration to leave us both feeling alive, and feeling extraordinary.

Weekly Practice

> *Create a celebration ritual. Use your celebration ritual at least once this week for an accomplishment of yours or of coworkers. Keep in mind that sometimes even the seemingly small things are HUGE.*

Selected Resources

Beavan, Colin. "Christmas With No Presents?", *Yes! Magazine*, 31 October 2008. Accessed 12/14/08. www.yesmagazine.org/article.asp?id=3042.

Deal, Terrence, and M.M. Key. *Corporate Celebration; Play, Purpose, and Profit at Work.* P. 5. San Francisco: Berrett-Koehler Publishers, 1998.

gthankyou.com (7/29/08 blog post) "Learning to Celebrate," Posted on July 29, 2008, by Rick Kiley

Smith, Sydney (3 June 1771–22 February 1845) English writer and Anglican cleric. Quote found at http://thinkexist.com /quotation/the_thing_about_performance-even_if_it-s_only_an/219814.html

Peters, Thomas J. (American Author and Consultant, b.1942) Quote found at http://thinkexist.com/quotation/celebrate_what_you_want_to_see_more_of/264684.html

Part 3:
Getting Along

Silence

Silence is one of the great arts of conversation.

—Marcus Tullius Cicero

> Yogic sages say that all the pain of a human life is caused by words, as is all the joy. We create words to define our experience and those words bring attendant emotions that jerk us around like dogs on a leash. We get seduced by our own mantras (I'm a failure I'm lonely I'm a failure I'm lonely) and we become monuments to them. To stop talking for a while, then, is to attempt to strip away the power of words, to stop choking ourselves with words, to liberate ourselves from our suffocating mantras.
>
> —Elizabeth Gilbert, *Eat, Pray, Love*

I wondered what a silent interaction with Darwin, a gothic squirrel monkey who weighs less than two pounds, would be like. He gets extremely excited (in more ways than one) when I come around to greet him in the morning, making himself quite big (in more ways than one) and squealing loudly and continuously while I talk to him. I usually say something like, "Oh yes, Darwin, I know you are 'The Man.' Mr. Macho Man, Mr. New York City boy." Before he came to live at the sanctuary, Darwin lived in New York City. New York's energy and confidence are a perfect fit for his own.

But on this morning I decided to try a different approach. I said, "Good morning, Darwin; good morning, Darrow." Darrow, another gothic squirrel monkey, is Darwin's girl—his roommate and life partner. I then just stood in silence and put my finger to my lips to signal, "Shhhhh."

Darwin

Then the most amazing thing happened. Darwin became quiet. His body eased into a relaxed state. I put my hands out to him. He licked them twice, and then he put his hands in mine. For the first time ever, in spite of the warning sign that says "Darwin Bites," Darwin and I touched hands.

Then something else happened. Darrow, who usually makes off to a corner hiding place when I'm around, also came over and touched my hands. She herself wasn't silent, but my silence seemed to invite an interaction.

Darrow

I remembered Bob Duggan, president of the Tai Sophia Institute for the Healing Arts, speaking to his students about ways to handle conflict in relationships. He offered this as a possibility: if you and your partner (lover, friend, office mate) find that you cannot agree on something and harsh words or accusations are arising, try an agreed silence. "I care about you. I can see that words are not working here. Let's agree to two days of silence." The time period of the agreed silence might be for one day, or even three or four days.

Agreed silence is *not* the same thing as "the silent treatment." The important thing is that the two individuals in disagreement have agreed to the amount of time to be in silence *before* the silence begins.

In *Material Success Through Yoga Principles,* Swami Kriyananda says:

> There is a close connection between the tongue and the brain. The more one can keep the tongue completely relaxed, the clearer he will find his mind become. A wagging tongue takes energy away from the brain and makes deep thinking difficult
>
> Mahatma Gandhi made a practice of setting aside one day a week when he simply wouldn't speak. Considering that an entire country depended on him, it must have been a challenge for him to keep that resolution. The result was, however, that he accomplished a great deal more than he could otherwise. He wrote letters, for instance, and composed public statements. People respected his silence and accommodated themselves to it. It was his firmness in adhering to resolutions like this that gave him the strength to sway millions to his will, and in the end, to force the British to withdraw from India. [Article accessed on line]

Silence is a powerful, yet gentle, way to create space for change. "Shhhhhh, Darwin. Let us just *be* together." Need I say more?

Weekly Practice

> *How might you use agreed silence to clear the way for change in your work life? Can you think of a situation where an impasse has been reached and an agreed silence might create the space for something new to emerge? Using the examples from the story above, create the practice for silence this week.*

Selected Resources

Gilbert, Elizabeth. *Eat, Pray, Love*. New York: Penguin Group, 2006.

Kriyananda, Swami. "Material Success Through Yoga Principles." [Article accessed on line at yoganandainstitute.org]

Guests

This being human is a guest house
every morning a new arrival.
A joy, a depression, a meanness,
some momentary awareness comes
as an unexpected visitor.
Welcome and entertain them all!
Even if they are a crowd of sorrows,
who violently sweep your house
empty of its furniture,
still treat each guest honorably.
He may be clearing you out for some new delight.
The dark thought, the shame, the malice,
meet them at the door laughing,
and invite them in.
Be grateful for whoever comes,
because each has been sent
as a guide from beyond.

—Rumi, "The Guest House"
(Translation by Coleman Barks, *The Essential Rumi*, 1995)

In February 2010, Maryland experienced two record-breaking snowfalls within the same week. In my town, about four and a half feet blanketed the ground, making every neighbor's yard look as good as the next.

On Day One of the first blizzard, many people stayed inside because shoveling seemed futile. The snow seemed to be accumulating as fast as a person could shovel. When the first blizzard ended on Day Two, people starting coming out to work on their driveways. But you couldn't walk over to chat, because you couldn't get there. By Day Three, a few paths had been dug between neighbors' houses. The neighbors on our right had lost their electricity. They didn't take us up on our offer to sleep in beds in a warm house, but they did dig the "Super Bowl Trail" between our houses to make sure they could get to our house for the big game!

That trail, along with others like it, were a vital part of all of us keeping our sanity. We still didn't have access to the road and hadn't seen a plow in a couple of days. We were hungry for companionship. So were all the other snowed-in Marylanders—Facebook was hopping. Most people were in complaint mode, feeling victimized by Mother Nature. In Maryland, being snowed in is such a rare occurrence that people didn't know how to just *be* with it. We are called *human beings*, but most of us are far from it. We are mostly *human doings*.

During the storms, I checked in by phone at least twice a day with Frisky's to make sure everyone was okay. Colleen and Scott still had seventy-five animals to care for, with many of them living in outside enclosures. They certainly couldn't just sit and *be* with the storm. The animals' lives depended on Colleen's and Scott's abilities to get out and feed them and give them water. It was a herculean effort for just two people to dig trails to reach everyone and make sure all the animals were still secure and the enclosures were undamaged.

On about Day Three, while everyone was getting grouchier on Facebook and planning island getaways to warm, sunny places, Isadora decided to check on her terrain. She ventured out through her tunnel to the outdoor portion

Isadora

of her enclosure. (Isadora is a black and white capuchin monkey, born November 22, 1996). What was her reaction? She screamed right out loud at the snow! If she had been on Facebook, you would have seen some very upset posts from her!

Across the state of Maryland, conditions were so severe that many business owners had to shut down for a couple of days. Even if the owners could get to work, most of their staff and customers could barely get out their front doors. The governor urged people not to drive. In Washington, DC, federal agencies stayed closed for four consecutive days. Some counties and suburbs even pulled the plows off the roads because of unsafe conditions.

Reactions to all of this went from one end of the scale to the other. While some people were able to take advantage of this time to increase Internet sales and do some networking, others were worried, frustrated, antsy, or angry.

The truth is, on any typical day, snow or no snow, we can experience these same emotions. Feelings of worry, frustration, restlessness, and anger are unpleasant. Trying to ignore them can make them even worse. So how can we shift to more positive-feeling emotions when we're caught up in the midst of negative ones? Acknowledge them. Don't ignore them.

Emotions are like people—they just want to be recognized and heard. Until you give them this acknowledgment, they'll stick around. Imagine each one of your emotions as a guest that shows up at your house. Some you would like to have stay for a long time. With others, you want their visits to be brief.

Dianne Connelly, author, speaker, and co-founder of the Tai Sophia Institute, shares a practice for acknowledging unpleasant emotions in order to shift them to more pleasant ones. Let's say anger shows up as your guest today. You say, "Oh, hello, Anger. I know you. You've been here before. Come on in and we'll have a cup of tea together. But you can't stay all day. I'm expecting other guests."

It's amazing how quickly anger will leave once you've recognized and honored it as a guest dropping in for a short visit.

So when Isadora, our capuchin teacher in this chapter, screamed, she was just honoring one of her guests—and this guest did not stay all day.

Weekly Practice

> *Over the course of the next week, practice using Dianne Connelly's technique as described above. Especially for unpleasant emotions, acknowledge them by giving them a name and inviting them in for a short visit as an honored guest. To help you embody this practice even more fully, try writing out the invitation in your journal, using the wording recommended. Notice the amount of time each of your guests visit.*

Selected Resources

Rumi. *The Essential Rumi.* P. 109. Translations by Coleman Barks with John Moyne. New York: HarperCollins, 1995.

Without Sam

O for the touch of a vanished hand.

—Alfred Lord Tennyson

They had been together for the past twenty-two years, side by side, longer than the average marriage lasts these days. They were each the only monkey the other had ever known. They endured the death of their original owner and shared a traumatic move from one owner to another. They had a building all to themselves when they moved to the sanctuary. "They" are Sam, a blue guenon, and Jackie, a vervet guenon.

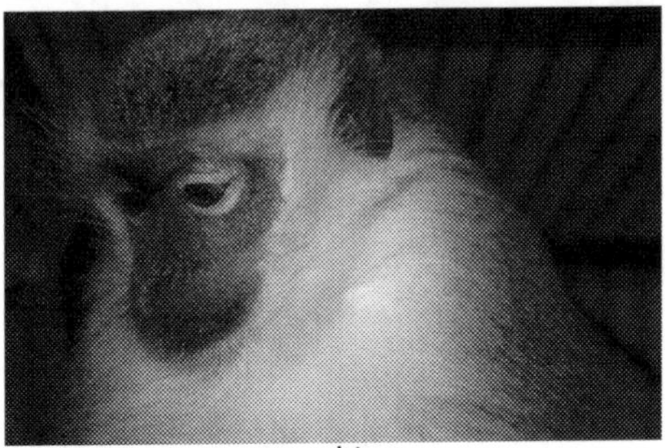

Jackie

As with most couples who have been together for a long time, the presence of the other was a comfort to each. Jackie loved to groom her Sam, which is a sign of affection among primates. Sam enjoyed watching Animal Planet, and Jackie loved her stuffed toys. She had about fifty, and she tended and groomed them as if they were the real babies she never had.

On the ninth day of February, in the year 2006, Sam took his last breath. He went to sleep and never awoke again for his beloved Jackie to groom. Afterward, Jackie was left to figure how to do life without Sam.

Sam

People who work together can also become extended family. When one dies, friends and co-workers grieve. These same feelings can be experienced during an economic recession. When some employees are laid off and some are left behind, the loss can be felt as deeply as a death. It can be hard to adapt to the new reality. The loss touches people's feelings about their work and the workplace, their lives outside of work, and their own fears about stability, death and dying. The feelings and symptoms of grief can take weeks, months, and even years to individually process. The brief time that most companies grant to attend a viewing and funeral only accommodates the very beginning stages of grief. The symptoms of grief and the ways we process it differ for each of us. They may include shock, denial, anger, guilt, anxiety, sleep disorders, exhaustion, overwhelming sadness, and problems with concentration.

Companies can do a great deal to help employees cope with their loss after the funeral. For example, co-workers can get together at a special lunch to share memories and feelings about the deceased. Bringing in someone from hospice to speak to the group may be helpful. Hospice offers a comprehensive program of care to patients and families facing a life-threatening illness, as well as bereavement counseling to help cope with the loss. A room could be named after the lost co-worker, and perhaps a ceremony held to honor the naming of the space. The annual company picnic could be named after the lost coworker, a fund could be established in the person's name, a tree could be planted on the company grounds the possibilities are unlimited. In these ways, the person can be remembered at a time of celebration, not only at a time of mourning.

One more thing to keep in mind is that people may need extra amounts of things that they needed before—healing treatment such as massage or acupuncture, a trip, or having a "cause" to work for to help others.

Most important is sensitivity to grieving staff members' needs. Patience is essential—there is no time limit on grieving. Don't make the assumption that they should be done grieving according to your timetable. Compassionate listening and acceptance are essential as well. There is no need to "fix" a grieving person's pain. Allowing grief to flow clears the way for healing to emerge.

Jackie is grooming her "babies" more than ever now. She's tucked so many into her bed box that we wonder how she fits herself in with them. It seems to bring her comfort when we let her show them to us, as if she has a story to tell about each one. Jackie reminds us that there is healing in tending to others, and healing in having another listen to your story. No fixing, just listening.

Weekly Practice

> *Be there for someone who is grieving or suffering. Listening is all that is required, so do not worry if you do not know what to say. A "yes," "wow," "hmm," or head nod is appropriate to let them know you are listening. Get rid of distractions. Make eye contact. Notice if you have the urge to "fix." But don't. Notice how the person responds to your listening.*

Selected Resources

McKay, Dawn Rosenberg. "Death in the Workplace: Dealing with the Death of a Co-worker." About.com. Accessed online 1/24/10 at http://careerplanning.about.com/od/personalissues/a/death.htm

The Patsy

To forgive is to set a prisoner free and discover that the prisoner was you.

—Lewis B. Smedes

She had been diagnosed with leukemia just weeks before. On the day of her transition from life here in the physical realm back to the realm of pure energy, or the "heavenly" realm, I had to transport her physical remains to a lab at Johns Hopkins Hospital in Baltimore. It was there that they performed a necropsy to confirm the cause of death. Our dear Patsy, a rhesus macaque, was just twenty-one years old. A rhesus macaque in captivity can live up to 40 years, and anywhere from 15 – 25 years in the wild.

Patsy

No matter how much we hated to see her suffer, there were still at least three broken hearts that day—mine, Colleen's, and Gizmo's. Colleen had spent the past fourteen years as Patsy's caregiver, and Gizmo, a male rhesus macaque, had spent the past fourteen years as Patsy's partner.

Upon my return to Frisky's that day, I asked Colleen if we could just sit for a little bit, drink a toast to Patsy, and share some fond memories and funny stories about our recently departed friend. Colleen's face lit with a smile, the first I had seen in two days.

"I remember getting the 'what for' from Patsy when she suspected that I'd come into her enclosure to remove a dirty toy for washing. She grabbed me by the shoulders and pushed me back and forth against the wall to let me know she was boss. Then she gently took her hand and caressed my face, as if to say, 'Honey, I'm sorry I had to do that to you. But you know I don't like you to just come in here and take my things away. I forgive you. You know I love you.'"

I affectionately named this method "The Patsy." I had to do the same thing to my husband when he drove off for the day with some timely materials that I needed that day and had to do without. I might add that it was a *visual* Patsy and not a physical one.

In an article titled "Forgiveness in the Workplace," writer Michael Stone addresses why forgiveness is so hard. Why can't we just tell the truth, make appropriate adjustments, and let go of resentments and past disappointments? According to Stone:

> One reason we do not practice forgiveness in the workplace is because we have very few role models to teach us how to do it. We find it is safer not to talk with people about the things they have done which have upset us, and for which we carry our resentments. It is more comfortable holding onto our grievances than confronting others. Our judgments keep us safe and separate, so that we don't have to deal with our own possible contribution to what we are having difficulty forgiving; or we might be avoiding similar actions and attitudes in ourselves.

Reverend Gussie Scardina, former assistant minister at The Columbia Center for Spiritual Living, says, "When you point a finger at someone, there are three pointing back at you." Go ahead—try it and you'll see what she means.

In *Happy Hour is 9 to 5,* author Alexander Kjerulf quotes Dr. Everett Worthington: "A tit-for-tat corporate culture can also lead to the loss of great workers." Dr. Worthington, a psychology professor at Virginia Commonwealth University, is also the executive director of the Campaign for Forgiveness Research. Worthington has studied more than one hundred workers in Virginia and Washington, DC, who were asked to recall incidents of workplace transgressions. "After conflicts, they no longer liked coming to work," Worthington said. "They became sicker and missed more work days. In some cases, they even changed jobs."

You do not need to become best friends with the person you feel let you down. Forgiveness is not about excusing the other person's behavior, and it is not about forgetting. It *is* about putting the incident behind you and moving on. Forgiveness is a powerful way to clear the negative energies you are holding on to, thus making way for real change. Forgiveness is for your own inner peace.

So the next time someone crosses you, visualize "The Patsy" and make a toast to one amazing monkey.

Weekly Practice

> *Take a blank sheet of paper and a pen or pencil. Without worrying about spelling or grammar, write for five to ten minutes about your anger around a situation and the person you are willing to work on forgiving for your own inner peace. Write hard or write big if you wish. After five minutes, tear up the paper into several pieces and then wad it up in a ball. Stomp on it several times with your foot. Pitch that paper into a trash bin or fireplace. Notice any relief you might feel. Repeat if necessary.*

Selected Resources

Kjerulf, Alexander. *Happy Hour is 9 to 5.* [http://positivesharing.com/happyhouris9to5/

Stone, Michael. "Forgiveness in the Workplace," Parts One and Two. *Lone Star Community.* Accessed online April 29, 2011. Part One: http://www.stc-dfw.org/newsletter/0304/1110.htm. Part Two: www.stc-dfw.org/newsletter/0305/1115.htm.

The Donkey

Who has seen the wind? Neither you nor I
but when the trees bow down their heads, the wind is passing by.

—Christina Rossetti

The donkey is known as a symbol of peace in the Christian faith. The donkey is frequently seen in the Nativity scene and in pictures of the Holy Family during their travels to Bethlehem. Jesus also made his triumphant entry through the gates of Jerusalem on the back of a donkey. Warriors and generals rode stallions, but Jesus was making his point that he was a humble peasant on a peace mission, not a warrior.

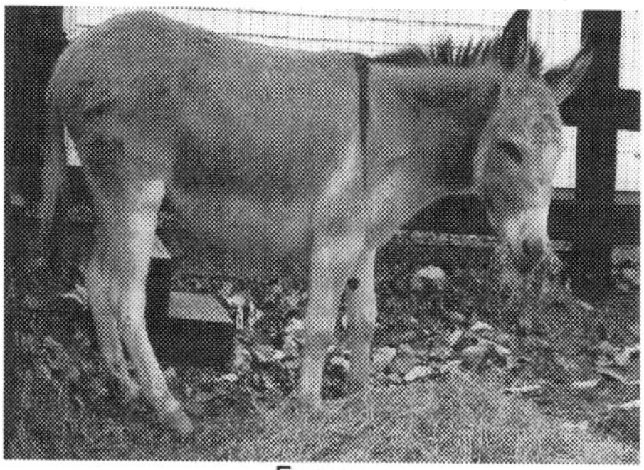

Eyore

But there was no peace in Woodstock, Maryland, when Eyore arrived at Frisky's. Eyore, the three-year-old donkey, arrived hee-hawing so loudly that no baby for miles around would have remained asleep.

Scotty Jr., a sixteen-pound vervet guenon monkey who had arrived at Frisky's twelve years earlier, was not buying into the "symbol of peace" bit at all! "There's not room for the two of us here! Get me my stallion! I want at him!" I could swear that's what Scotty Jr.'s loud monkey squeals sounded like, with antics to match.

Diana, another vervet guenon and Scotty Jr.'s female roommate, was also not taking this lightly. Was she reacting to the donkey, or to Scotty Jr.?

We had to start somewhere to restore the peace, so we sent Scotty off on a two-day meditative retreat. (Not really—we just kept him inside for two days.) And he came back a changed monkey. Apparently he'd done some deep thinking and realized that if the *ass* was here to stay, he needed to look at what they had in common: one, they both belonged to the animal kingdom; two, they both had a *key* behind their animal names; and three, their animal names rhymed. Okay, so he had to dig deep. And even though there was no more room at the inn, the donkey could stay down by the manger.

Scotty, Jr.

Scotty's approach can also be an effective practice for dealing with diversity issues in the workplace: start by looking for the similarities.

For example, occasionally there's someone you need to work with who is difficult. The Tai Sophia Institute has a simple yet profound practice whose purpose is to help us acknowledge our similarities. The Bow is one of the first practices that new students at the institute are taught. It is a ritual way of acknowledging one another, performed in complete silence.

I and five other Tai Sophia students stood in a circle. One at a time, each of us took a turn stepping into the center of the circle, looking each person in the eyes, and bowing. This is done individually to each person in the circle. The person who received the bow acknowledged "the gift received" with a Native American gesture that means just that—two taps over the heart with the side of a fisted hand, and a third tap with a flat hand over the heart. Once the recipient had acknowledged the gift had been received, the person in the center moved on to make eye contact with the next recipient, repeating the entire process. After bowing to everyone in the circle, the person in the center silently rejoined the circle, and the next person stepped into the center.

Never have I experienced such a powerful exercise in acknowledgment. Its power lies in honoring others *exactly as they are*. Such deep acknowledgment cuts through the superficial perception of differences that keeps us separate and clears the way for authentic connection.

Is there someone that you couldn't possibly acknowledge in this way? There may be times when, in order to find a similarity, you might have to go as deep as simply bowing to the fact that you and the other person are both human beings here on this earth together. Perhaps that person could be here to teach you tolerance or forgiveness. In *Turning to One Another,* author Margaret J. Wheatley writes: "We acknowledge each other as equals. What makes us equals is that we are human beings. A second thing that makes us equals is that we need each other. Whatever we know, it is not sufficient. We cannot see enough of the whole."

I snicker as I think about a scene in the movie *Night at the Museum*. Ben Stiller, who plays a night watchman at the museum, is being taunted by a monkey who continually steals his keys. The watchman is getting frustrated and quite angry at the monkey, until the wax figure of Teddy Roosevelt (played by Robin Williams) comes alive at night and asks Stiller's character, "Who's evolved?"

Stiller retorts, "I am!" as he watches Roosevelt easily get the keys back from the monkey.

So if there are times you find you have to dig deep to acknowledge someone with a bow, even if the bow is only in your mind, remember: if Scotty Jr. could do it, so can you. After all, "Who's evolved?"

Weekly Practice

Choose at least one person to receive a bow from you. You may tell them you are practicing acknowledgment this week. Ask first if they would be willing to receive a bow from you. Explain the signal for "gift received" that is explained in the chapter above, so they may give this back in return. What did you notice?

Selected Resources

Wheatley, Margaret J. *Turning to One Another: Simple Conversations to Restore Hope to the Future*. San Francisco: Berrett-Koehler Publishers, 2002.

Declaration

I have nothing to declare except my genius.

—Oscar Wilde

Kiko, a male rhesus macaque who weighs twenty-eight pounds on a good day, has both an indoor and outdoor enclosure. Inside he can watch Animal Planet on TV. Outside he can feel the breezes, visit with volunteers, or play on his swing. He can choose to be inside or outside whenever he pleases, thanks to a tunnel with a flap that swings both ways, keeping the cold outside in winter and the coolness inside in summer. There is one exception, though, to his freedom of choice: when Colleen needs to get into his enclosure to clean and replace bedding. To begin the cleaning process, she shuts off access to one side while she's cleaning the other. It's best for Colleen and Kiko to be separated during the cleaning process, because it makes Kiko mad to have his things rearranged. You'll understand this if you have a teenager or have ever raised one. Often you can get in to clean a teen's room only if he or she is not around.

Like many teenagers, monkeys tend to keep messy rooms, and they don't mind it a bit. However, to keep odors and flies at bay, we caregivers must get in regularly to keep things fresh. Colleen was beginning to feel very frustrated on this particular day, when she needed to get in and give Kiko's space a thorough cleaning and Kiko was just not going to allow it! She had tried everything that had worked in the past to get Kiko outside so she could slide the door shut, but to no avail. Kiko was on to us. He watched us with a suspicious look, knowing we were not there just to visit this time. Capable of movements much quicker than ours, he stood his ground and outsmarted every one of our brilliant plans.

Kiko

With most people, when change is forced upon us, fear kicks in. Our routines and activities that have felt comfortable and familiar now require conscious thought. Our "animal instinct" at these times is to defend our comfort zone. It seemed to me that this was what was happening with Kiko when we came to take away his bedding and dirty toys and replace them with new ones.

As human primates, we tend to be quite practiced at resistance, especially when it comes to change in the workplace. In his article "Why Do People Resist Change?" Douglas Firebaugh states:

> Mainly when change has entered a person's life in the past, it usually came in the form of a loss, not a gain (at least in our version of reality).
>
> It is carried with Pain, not Pleasure.
>
> And most people equate change to something negative, versus positive.

More often than not, clearing the way for change is a matter of attitude. Tom Balles, author of *Dancing With The Ten Thousand Things: Ways to Become a Powerful Healing Presence*, reminds us that our words have power: "If you say it is not worth the effort, then it isn't. If you say nothing will ever change, most likely it never will. The antidote to helplessness is your *declaration*. By your declaration, new possibilities have a chance to come into being." (p. 162)

So after a few days of Kiko's resistance, Colleen *declared* that today would be easy. This time when she went out to Kiko, she asked him for his help. "Honey, please, I really could use your help. I just don't know what to do. Please let me know how to make this easier for you. I need to clean your room so that you can stay healthy. I'm not doing this to be mean." This time, Kiko cooperated.

Philosopher Johann Wolfgang von Goethe's words about the power of committing to a decision apply equally well to the idea of making a declaration:

> The moment one definitely commits oneself, then Providence moves, too. All sorts of things occur to help one that would never otherwise have occurred. A whole stream of events issues from the decision, raising in one's favor all manner of unforeseen incidents and meetings and material assistance which no man could have dreamt would have come his way.

Weekly Practice

> *What declaration will you make to clear the way for results?*

Selected Resources

Balles, Tom. *Dancing with the Ten Thousand Things: Ways to Become a Powerful Healing Presence*. Bloomington, IN: iUniverse 2004.

von Goethe, Johann Wolfgang. [German writer, drawer, and philosopher, 28 August 1749–22 March 1832] Quote accessed online 9/12/11 at http://www.spiritandflesh.com/textCommitmentGoethecreationprovidencewill.htm

Part 4: Communicating with Awareness

Being Disturbed

Trauma is nothing more than being stuck in what you believe.

—Byron Katie

Being the keeper of the main house on this particular day, I got up from the computer to stretch my legs and walked into the monkey room to check on my little pals. All was calm. We had already said our hellos when I first arrived, which is usually a high-energy activity. It's very similar to when we greet human friends we haven't seen in a while: we hug, we smile, we raise our eyebrows, and we tend to have a heightened burst of energy in our voices. After the initial greeting, we adjust to the new presence and our bodies tend to return to a more relaxed state.

Squeaky

I entered the section where the squirrel monkeys are located. With the exception of Darwin, a 1.8 pound gothic squirrel monkey who loves to exhibit to the females just how manly he is, everyone was quiet. They were used to his "macho" act. I stood still for a few moments talking to Darwin. I never heard a peep out of the others.

Then, for what seemed to me to be no apparent reason, chaos broke loose. Squeaky jumped on Nicole, who let out a "get off me!" type of squeal. This set off shrill squealing from all of the others. My jaw dropped, my eyebrows went up, my body tensed, and I thought, "What did I do? I must have done something to cause all of this!"

Sometimes in the workplace, we notice ourselves becoming disturbed by something that someone said, did, or did not do. In *Turning to One Another: Simple Conversations to Restore Hope to the Future,* author Margaret J. Wheatley asks us to take on a practice:

> Noticing what surprises and disturbs me has been a very useful way to see invisible beliefs. If what you say surprises me, I must have been assuming something else was true. If what you say disturbs me, I must believe something contrary to you. My shock at your position exposes my own position. When I hear myself saying, "How could anyone believe something like that?" a light comes on for me to see my own beliefs. These moments are great gifts. If I can see my beliefs and assumptions, I can decide whether I still value them.
>
> Begin a conversation, listening for what's new. Listen as best you can for what's different, for what surprises you. See if this practice helps you to learn something new. Notice whether you develop a better relationship with the person you're talking with. (p. 36)

Squeaky and Nicole helped me to see that I had made an assumption—that I was somehow the cause of this upset among the squirrel monkeys. The new awareness for me was that there could have been thousands of other factors that I could not see or hear, of which only they were aware.

Becoming aware of our own assumptions is the first step in communicating more authentically, whether in our work relationships or our personal lives. Thank you, Squeaky and Nicole. You are my teachers.

Weekly Practice

> *When something disturbs you, write down these questions: What are my underlying beliefs and assumptions that led me to being disturbed by this situation or person? What have I noticed about my own unspoken values and beliefs? Sit in silence for a while. Stay away from the computer and sending texts until you have some insight.*

Selected Resources

Wheatley, Margaret J. *Turning to One Another: Simple Conversations to Restore Hope to the Future.* P. 36. San Francisco: Berrett-Koehler Publishers, 2002.

Thief

Ever since Eve gave Adam the apple,
there has been a misunderstanding between the sexes about gifts.

—Nan Robertson

I used to be able to give her a backrub. In fact, she was the only squirrel monkey who seemed to ask for physical interaction with me. Zoey, the tiniest of all the monkeys at Frisky's, suffered from Crohn's disease and weighed just less than one pound. Cocoa, another female squirrel monkey and Zoey's companion, weighed nearly a whopping two pounds, a normal size for a squirrel monkey. They came to Frisky's together in 1997. When their original owners got divorced, their new life situations didn't allow for their pets.

Zoey

When Colleen noticed an increasing amount of aggression between Cocoa and Zoey, she made the decision to separate them for a while, pushing the divider panel shut in the middle of their enclosure. That's when Zoey began to invite backrubs, leaning up for the soothing relief of touch that my fingers would bring to her through the bars that separated us. I enjoyed being able to give comfort to this frail little being.

After a four-month separation, Colleen reopened the divider panel to allow the old companions to interact with each other once again and move freely between both sides of the enclosure. I was happy to see the two back together, knowing their world had been expanded.

The trade-off for me was not being able to give Zoey backrubs any longer. Whenever I made the attempt, Cocoa would rush down in an agitated state to make sure I didn't touch Zoey. "Jealous thief" was what I often thought, because I felt as if Cocoa had stolen my opportunity to be able to touch Zoey anymore.

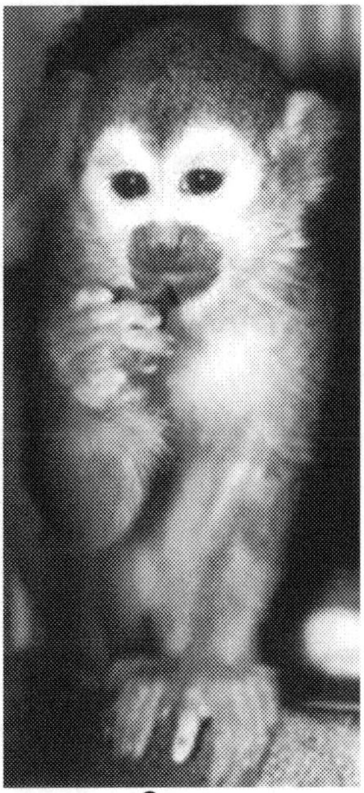
Cocoa

Soon afterward, I stumbled across a story I'd seen once before in *Chicken Soup for the Soul*. In "The Cookie Thief," a story by Valerie Cox written in verse, a woman had some extra time at the airport before her flight. She bought a book and a bag of cookies at an airport shop and found a place to settle down to read until her flight was ready to board. She reached into the bag of cookies, which was between her and the man sitting next to her. Then she saw the man reach into the bag and also take a cookie. "How rude," she thought to herself, but said nothing in order to avoid a scene. She reached for another, and then he reached for one, too. She could hardly believe this man. "Thief! Ingrate!" she thought. This kept on until there was only one cookie left in the bag. "I wonder what he'll do now," she fumed to herself. He took the last cookie, broke it in half, and handed the other half to her. She snatched it from him, never having been so galled in all her life. Her flight was finally called and she headed to the gate, refusing to look back at this thief who had stolen her cookies. Once she was seated, she reached into her tote bag to find her book—and gasped with surprise. There inside her tote was her bag of cookies, not yet opened. "Oh, no!" she thought. "If my cookies are still here, then *I'm* the one who stole his—and he shared his cookies with me!" (p. 199)

How many times has each of us misjudged a situation? The timing of this story coming my way for a second time couldn't have been more perfect. Colleen had called me earlier that same day to tell me something about Cocoa and Zoey. "I have to tell you what I just witnessed," she said. "Zoey has been pretty lethargic for the past three days, and right now Cocoa is holding Zoey in her arms and rubbing her back. It's just so touching to see how Cocoa protects and tends to Zoey." My eyes filled with tears as my story of "jealous thief" transformed into a story of protection and tender loving care. Was it coincidence that this story turned up twice in my life? I don't think so.

How much difference might it make in our own lives and the lives of those around us if we learned to reframe our stories of imagined wrongdoings and resentment? Authentic communication includes the ability to tell a different story, and it's a skill that is vital to being an effective leader or businessperson. In his book *Unlimited Power,* author Anthony Robbins shares an anecdote about Tom Watson, the founder of IBM. Watson is a master at "reframing" or "telling a different story."

> One of Watson's employees had made a mistake that cost the company $10 million. Watson called the employee into his office, and the employee said, "I suppose you want my resignation." Watson replied, "Are you kidding? We just spent $10 million educating you!" (p. 312)

There's *always* Another Way To See It.

Weekly Practice

> *Phenomenon is an observation or fact. Story is what we make up about that phenomenon based on our assumptions and beliefs. For example, in the cookie thief story, the man was eating*

cookies from the same bag as the woman. That is a phenomenon. Story is "the man is rudely helping himself to cookies from the woman's bag." Choose an upset in the workplace or in your personal life. Write down the phenomenon. Practice telling a different story and notice any relief this brings to your body or to the situation.

Selected Resources

Canfield, Jack and Mark Victor Hansen. *A 3rd Serving of Chicken Soup for the Soul: 101 More Stories to Open the Heart and Rekindle the Spirit.* P. 199. Health Communications Inc., Deerfield Beach, FL, 1996.

Robbins, Anthony, *Unlimited Power: The New Science of Personal Achievement.* P. 312. Free Press, a division of Simon and Schuster, Inc., 1986, New York, NY

Do or Do Not

There are only two options regarding commitment. You're either in or out. There's no such thing as a life in-between.

—Pat Riley

"Jackie, may I see your baby?" She picks up one of her beloved stuffed animals, brings it a little closer to me, and begins to groom it. She treats it with such care that we believe she is caring for the little one that she never had, talking to it like a mama talks to her baby. She's not speaking any human language, of course—Jackie is a vervet guenon monkey. But it is clear that she is communicating, and that she is answering my request.

Nikki

"Gizmo, will you come outside and let me say hello?" I can hear that he has his TV on in the comfort of his climate-controlled indoor/outdoor enclosure. Within seconds, Gizmo, a rhesus macaque, opens the flap to his tunnel and comes outside. It's clear to me that he answered my request.

"Nikki, will you come over and let me say hello?" Nikki, a female gothic squirrel monkey, makes no move to come closer or acknowledge me with eye contact. If she had given even a glance in my direction, I would have thought, "Maybe she's thinking about it but isn't yet fully committed. Perhaps she's trying." But it was clear—she was not answering my request.

In each case above, the answer was clear. Each monkey either honored my request or did not honor my request. But when a request or invitation is made to us, we humans have a third answer that is very overused: "I'll try." It's a cop-out, a noncommitment, often used to blow someone off when we don't want to hurt their feelings by saying no. However, people more often feel disappointed when we say we'll "try" and then don't accomplish what was asked. Authentic communication depends on our speaking with *both* honesty and sensitivity.

In her article "'I'll Try' Doesn't Fly!", author Cookie Tuminello, founder of Success Source, LLC, a team-building company, has this to say about the use of the word *try*:

> How many times a day do you hear yourself or others use the phrase, "I'll try ... to get this project done" or "I'll try ... to come to the meeting"? I cringe every time I hear it. My clients however, know that saying, "I'll try" does not fly with me. Here are three thoughts that come up for me when someone says, "I'll try ..." Are you afraid to commit, afraid to say NO, or afraid you won't succeed so you want to leave a back door open just in case?
>
> By copping out and using the "I'll try" response, you're admitting that you aren't committed to doing the necessary work to be the person you want to be in your life. When you live your life mired in mediocrity, you get mediocre results.

One of the most famous lines in the movie *Star Wars V: The Empire Strikes Back* comes from Jedi Master Yoda when he asks the young Luke Skywalker to remove his spacecraft from the swamp even though it looks impossible.

Skywalker, quite skeptical, replies, "I'll try." Master Yoda was quick to teach and replied sternly, "Do, or do not. There is no try."

Sure, there are times when it might be appropriate to use the word try. If someone asks you to taste a food you've never eaten before, you might say, "Sure, I'll try a piece." If you're asked to do something that is outside of your expertise or comfort zone, such as bungee jumping, you might say, "Sure, I'll give it a try," just to let the person know that you're a beginner—not practiced, but willing to take the challenge. You know the difference between the taking-the-challenge "try" and the *I'm-blowing-you-off* "try."

Jackie, Gizmo, Nikki, and Yoda have eliminated the concept of "trying" altogether. For these Masters, it is "Do or Do Not."

Weekly Practice

> *Notice how often you are tempted to use the word* try *(or how often you actually do use it!). Each time, substitute an authentic response instead. For example, if someone asks you, "Will you come to the meeting on Wednesday?" and you're not yet ready to make the commitment, substitute something like, "No. I won't be there," or "I'll let you know for sure by Tuesday." And then let them know yes or no by Tuesday.*

Selected Resources

Tuminello, Cookie. "'I'll Try' Doesn't Fly." *SelfGrowth.com*. Accessed online 9/24/10. http://www.selfgrowth.com/articles/I_ll_Try_Doesn_t_Fly.html.

Both-And

Both optimists and pessimists contribute to our society.
The optimist invents the airplane and the pessimist the parachute.

—G. B. Stern

Cindy Lou, a one pound, ten ounce gothic squirrel monkey, did not look right. She was sitting with her eyes closed, which is not the usual behavior I see when I do the rounds at the sanctuary. Usually, the room fills with a heightened sense of awareness when someone walks in.

I stood watching Cindy Lou with some concern. With her eyes still closed, she crouched over, made fists, and laid her forehead against them. I knew she couldn't answer back with words, but I asked her anyway, "Cindy Lou, are you okay?"—even though I knew the answer. One look at her and even the untrained eye could see that she was not okay. A few moments later, looking as if she was completely hungover, she climbed up into her bed box.

An hour and a half later, Colleen returned from running errands and noticed the same symptoms. Her assessment as an experienced primate caregiver was that Cindy Lou was in pain. Colleen was able to get Cindy Lou to take some Infants' Tylenol to reduce the pain. She also contacted Dr. Keith Gold of Chadwell Animal Hospital in Abingdon, Maryland, Frisky's primate care veterinarian. Colleen reached him just in time—he was leaving for Disney World the next day. Being the wonderful hero to Frisky's that he is, he told Colleen to bring Cindy Lou in immediately. It turned out that she had two broken teeth, one of which had abscessed. Dr. Gold removed one tooth and performed a root canal on the other. Two days later, a very relieved Cindy Lou was eating papaya like it was going out of style!

Cindy Lou

From the interaction with Cindy Lou, I am reminded just how much of our communication depends on our awareness of body language. One of the ways this shows up in today's business world is in teleconferences, which have become so prevalent. I struggle with them, because it's impossible to read body language and facial expressions over the phone, and I'm never quite sure when to jump into the conversation. Sue Knight's book *NLP at Work: The Difference That Makes a Difference in Business* sheds some light on this challenge:

> Over the telephone, we can find low levels of response to what we say disconcerting. We might misread it as disinterest. It is hard to tell when we can't read the body language to go along with it.
>
> By reading body language signals, we can know when to end a conversation, read whether or not people understand what you said, determine the level of agreement we have achieved, tell when we have established a connection, tell if someone is engaged in the conversation or distracted. (p. 66)

On the phone, we can't know whether someone is about to speak, just as we can't know when someone isn't feeling good. We can't know whether a silence on the other end of the phone line means that the other person is formulating a thoughtful answer or that they've tuned out and are going through their e-mail during the call.

To be fair, as much as I dislike teleconferencing, it also has advantages. It may feel more comfortable for some people to talk on the phone rather than meeting in person. Also, when in-person meetings aren't feasible, teleconferences allow us to meet with people from all over the country, or even all over the world. In "The Teleconference: Top Ten Secrets to Hold a Successful One," e-zine writer Nathalie Fiset offers some helpful tips, which are summarized below:

Identify yourself before you speak. It often is not easy to discern which voice belongs to whom, even when you have met the speaker before. Simply say, "Heather's speaking." (Of course, fill in your own name if it isn't Heather.)

Take turns. Make sure each participant is heard and understood. Limit the number of open-ended questions that are asked of the group in order to keep the meeting within the intended time frame. For example, asking the question "Does anyone have an opinion?" could start the entire group talking at once. It could also have the opposite reaction and create awkward silence. Ask specific people what they think so you can receive individual responses.

Use your voice. Learning to use proper intonation and volume will help emphasize points in the statements you make. Keep in mind, many teleconferences do not allow people to read body language or see facial expressions that may help make your point when you are face to face. In that case, your voice is your only tool in making sure that people understand the point you are trying to make.

When it comes to teleconferencing, I find myself in "either/or" thinking: it has to be either this way *or* that way ... I can have either this *or* that. In reality, practicing "both-and" thinking opens us up to so much more possibility. I don't have to choose to do all my meetings either in person or all my meetings by teleconference—I can live in a world of "both-and," learning to communicate both in person and by teleconference. Adapting in this way will certainly reduce my suffering. In *The Art of Possibility,* a story about one of the authors, Rosamund Stone Zander, makes a point about a challenge on the ski slopes.

Rosamund was alone on a three-day ski trip to concentrate on improving her skiing. On her first run down the mountain, she slipped and fell on a patch of ice. She found herself becoming resistant and tensing up whenever she spotted ice—and there was lots of it! She was thinking of abandoning the project and coming back at another time when real snow skiing was to be had. She then had an "Aha!" moment, realizing that she had been operating under the assumption that real skiing was on snow. She created a new story for herself; if she was going to be a real New England skier, she had better include ice in her definition of skiing. (p. 101)

Rosamund's story shows how the mind can get stuck in a story of how conditions must be. When she switched from the belief that "either the ice goes or I go" to "I can learn to ski on both snow *and* ice by adjusting my method," a new possibility was born.

Aha! If I am going to be an effective communicator, I had better include teleconferences in my definition of effective communication. And, thanks to little Cindy Lou, I will promise to keep my "reading body language" skills polished!

Weekly Practice

> *Notice situations where "either/or" thinking is prevalent and transform it to a "both-and" conversation.*

Selected Resources

Knight, Sue. *NLP at Work: The Difference That Makes a Difference in Business.* P. 66. Nicholas Brealey Publishing, London, UK, 2002.

Zander, Rosamund Stone and Benjamin Zander. *The Art of Possibility.* P. 101. New York: Penguin Books, 2000.

Fiset, Nathalie, "The Teleconference: Top Ten Secrets to Hold a Successful One." Accessed online June 2, 2010 at http://ezinearticles.com/?The-Teleconference---Top-Ten-Secrets-to-Hold-a-Successful-One&id=1018860

The Power of No

The most important thing in communication
is to hear what isn't being said.

—Peter F. Drucker

We were holding hands and making faces and silly sounds at one another. Isadora, a six and a half pound, black and white capuchin monkey, and I were having all sorts of fun and the others wanted a part of it! When I decided it was time to spread the spirit of fun to the others, I started to pull away. But Isadora wasn't finished with me yet, so she tightened her grip on me. I figured a firm "*No,* Isadora!" would make her come to her senses and loosen her grip. Wrong! She then dug in with her fingernails. As I gave a "you tricky little stinker" sort of laugh, I could hear Colleen call out from the other room, "Never say no to a monkey!"

Isadora

As it is with monkeys, humans are powerfully struck by the word *no.* That tiny little word can send any two-year-old into a full-blown tantrum and drive many teenagers into rebellious acts of "I'll show you!" I'm reminded of what happened during the 2005–2006 school year. Seven local high school students showed up drunk to a school dance after the school had spent the entire week leading up to the dance saying (and drawing attention to) "*No* drinking, *no* drinking." The continuous threat of *no* seemed to be only an invitation to be challenged. The kids already knew what the rules were. Could taunting have invited rebellion? Could the overuse of *no* have played a part in this?

Bob Duggan, founder and president of the Tai Sophia Institute, opened the doors to this renowned institute of acupuncture and healing arts in 1975, long before acupuncture was a household word. He did so despite negativity from nonbelievers. Now this accredited school draws people from all over the country to its three successful master's degree programs. Tai Sophia is a preeminent academic institution for wellness-based education, clinical care, research, and public policy discourse. Integration of eastern and western thinking has empowered and transformed individuals, organizations, and communities. Duggan says, "This place wouldn't exist if I'd stopped at the first person who said it wouldn't work. I found another way around it."

The word *no* can be like running into a brick wall for some people when they find themselves unable to move forward or get around it. Gary, a thirty-nine-year-old father who was once married, became so used to hearing the words "No, you can't do that" after his brain injury that he now believes that to be the truth. His conversation is full of constant references to his "low IQ," and he has difficulty holding a job. Yet his "low IQ" is not apparent in talking with him.

How many times have you or someone you work with said no and shut down all possibility? How many in the organization are affected by that answer? In order to keep life moving forward in any conversation or meeting, it may serve to be in the practice of "Request, Accept, Decline, or Counteroffer." The first step in using this practice is to realize that every upset, concern, complaint, or conflict is actually a Request in disguise. When someone is complaining, ask that person if he or she is actually making a Request. If the answer is yes, ask the person to word it in the form of a Request so you can be clear about what they are requesting. This step is important if the intent is to remain in partnership. Then follow with the remaining steps:

- Once the person's Request has been spoken, others who may also be part of the conversation have the option to Accept, Decline, or Counteroffer.
- If there are only one or two Declines in a big group, ask if they have a Counteroffer.
- If there is no Counteroffer, ask if they are *willing to let it go.*
- If the person who made the Request is not willing to accept a Decline as an option, then it is important to realize that this was not a Request at all, but a Demand.

Once a group is practiced in the art of Request, demands can be used sparingly. Remember, the word *no* can *open up* or *shut down* all possibility.

"Isadora, I request that you give me back my fingers," I said. She counteroffered with her tail, and I eventually had to decline.

Weekly Practice

Identify where a complaint may be a Request in disguise and use the exercise in this chapter.

Selected Resources

"Request, Accept, Decline, or Counteroffer." This practice was learned in the Applied Helaing Arts Program at the Tai Sophia Institute in Laurel, MD in 2005.

Uh-Uh

Today the fate of humankind is even more crucially linked than ever before. The boundaries between the problems of "others" and "our" problems are being increasingly erased.

—Janez Drnovsek

"To cross the line" is a phrase we use to communicate that something has changed from being acceptable to being unacceptable. For example, when we have crossed the line with a dog, the first sign we might observe is a growl. If we don't back off, the next thing we might see is a snarl, with teeth showing. If we still don't back off, we'll probably get bitten.

When we cross the line with a monkey, we may see a number of different warning signals, with the type of signals depending on the breed. Often, the monkey will exhibit a "warrior-like" stance, stillness, and a stare. The jaw may drop, leaving the canine teeth displayed. Some monkeys will jump to the back of the enclosure to avoid confrontation. Others will come to the front of the enclosure and grab the bars. These are all clear warning signals. If you move closer, you might be grabbed through the bars, scratched, or bitten.

Dawson, a Java macaque (born April 2001), lunges forward when he feels threatened. He'll grab the bars and start shaking them. Any sensible human knows that this means, "Back off!" The sign above his enclosure reads, "No Visitors Allowed in Here." Funnily enough, Dawson will actually grab the sign and shake it. How's that for clarity? He has done this so often that the sign is showing signs of wear on the sides. He'll stop the aggression if the visitor simply moves out of the room.

Darwin

Humans can certainly cross lines with other humans. Humor is a human behavior that can easily cross the line into unacceptability. For all its capacity to unite, it can also quickly become divisive if not used with sensitivity.

Should the use of humor at work ever be off limits? As keynote speaker and author of *Inspiring Workplaces* and *You Can't Be Serious!—Putting Humor to Work* , Michael Kerr says it's one of the most common questions he gets:

"It's not an easy question to answer because humor is such a wide-ranging and subjective topic. One person's funny is another person's offensive, cruel, downright stupid, insensitive comment."

"And we need to remind ourselves of how powerful a resource humor is. How humor, when used effectively (and there's the kicker) has helped people throughout history cope with wars and death and tragedy, sometimes in the most unspeakably horrific circumstances."

"But, having said all that, the flip side is that we all know that humor can be used to bully people and that inappropriate remarks under the guise of humor can be devastatingly cruel and offensive. Humor CAN build walls between people, as easily as it can sometimes tear down walls."

In November 2009, I attended World Laughter Tour's Advanced Laughter Leader Workshop in Columbus, Ohio. Steve Wilson, a psychologist, psychotherapist, and founder of World Laughter Tour, gave a lecture entitled "Putting Up With Put-Down Humor." He shared a story about a group gathered for a meeting.

To evoke some laughter, the group leaders began by telling jokes that poked fun at the state of Kentucky. After a few jokes, Kevin, one of the meeting participants, was not laughing. He simply voiced, "Uh-uh." The joking subsided, and everyone turned to Kevin. He explained that "Uh-uh" is the warning signal he uses when someone has "crossed the line." Kevin had an emotional connection with the state of Kentucky. The group had no idea that they had crossed the line with Kevin. You see, the line is invisible. People don't usually cross it on purpose. Nobody said, "What's the matter, you can't take a joke?" Responding in this way makes one a "Humor Abuser." A Humor Abuser blames the victim. The group respected Kevin's view and discontinued the jokes about Kentucky. Steve ended the story by saying, "Kevin raised the group's consciousness."

Humor can be either constructive or destructive. Here are some guidelines to consider before using humor in your workplace:

Humor is destructive when it:

- lowers self-esteem
- belittles someone
- perpetuates a stereotype
- closes off creative thought
- stimulates laughter *at* someone
- creates defensiveness
- excludes someone

Humor is constructive when it:

- includes people
- reduces tension
- stimulates laughter *with* someone
- breaks down barriers

- stimulates new ideas
- is supportive
- creates a positive atmosphere

World Laughter Tour trains people in leading and creating positive environments. The methods used are not based on joke-telling but on a nonthreatening, playful approach. The playful movements done with laughter are called laughter exercises. Mirthful laughter offers many benefits that not only encourage authentic communication but also support self-esteem and wellness: people connect and experience a sense of belonging and cooperation; catecholamines (which are known to boost mental function) increase; mood is elevated through the release of endorphins; blood pressure is lowered; cortisol (the stress hormone) levels are decreased; and immune system efficiency is increased.

Numerous other physical and emotional benefits result from laughter. Scientific studies have confirmed that oxytocin, also known as "the bonding hormone," is released when we laugh *with* others. Professor Gareth Leng, a neuroscientist at the University of Edinburgh, says, "Oxytocin and endorphins have been associated with reduction in stress, and they encourage social and sexual interaction." A study done by Thomas Baumgartner at the University of Zurich Center for Study of Social and Neural Systems showed that oxytocin also increases levels of trust. Perhaps this is why people feel connected when they laugh together.

Using jokes in the workplace to induce laughter can be very risky business. Steve Wilson says, "There are two sure rules for making something funny—however, nobody knows what they are." When someone crosses the line, trust is threatened. The dog growls, Darwin grabs the bars and displays his canines, Kevin says, "Uh-uh."

What is your warning signal?

Weekly Practice

> *Pay attention to the use of humor. Notice if its characteristics are constructive or destructive. Notice how these two types of humor are received. Do you know the group or person's background well enough to take the risk with destructive humor?*

Selected Resources

Kerr, Michael, "Humor in the Workplace: Should Humor at Work EVER be Off Limits?" September 26, 2010, article accessed on line January 11, 2012, at http://www.mikekerr.com/humour-at-work-blog/humor-in-the-workplace-when-should-humor-at-work-ever-be-off-limits/

Constructive Humor vs. Destructive Humor, from the "How to Create Therapeutic Laughter and Laughter Clubs" training manual, 2000–2009, WLT, Inc., www.worldlaughtertour.com, originated as handout from Karyn Buxman, www.karynbuxman.com

Baumgartner, Thomas, of Zurich, Center for Study of Social and Neural Systems. Study information accessed online 2/11/10 at www.cell.com/neuron/retrieve/pii/S0896627308003279

Leng, Gareth, Neouroscientist at the University of Edinburgh, quoted in article by Mairi Macleod, 10/15/05, "Laughter beats hunting fleas." Accessed online 9/7/09 http://www.nzherald.co.nz/world/news/article.cfm?c_id=2&objectid=10350316

Simply Speaking

It is more fun to talk with someone who doesn't use long, difficult words but rather short, easy words like "What about lunch?"

—A. A. Milne, *Winnie-the-Pooh*

My beloved, intelligent husband, Bob, can tell when he has given me an explanation that goes way beyond my level of understanding or what I want to know. My eyes start to glaze over. I look down at my toes and begin to ponder whether I'm ready for my next pedicure. I tap my knees and scratch my head. He has a background in electrical engineering; I have a master's degree in the applied healing arts. He likes to know how and why things work; I just want to know *that* they work and be amazed by the mystery of it all.

I like simple words and easy reads. One thing that I get a big kick out of is when a company's mission statement goes on with way too many sentences and "impressive" business vocabulary—the kind you have to read three times and you still think "huh?" According to the National Adult Literacy Survey, the average American adult reads at an eighth to ninth grade level. However, nearly 1 in 5 adults read at or below the fifth grade level, and nearly 2 out of 5 older Americans and minorities read at or below that level.

My good friend Willie, a ten pound, wedge-capped capuchin monkey, adores me. When he sees me, he squeals with delight and reaches for my hands. If he's eating, it doesn't matter. He stops eating and squeals and drools with the food still in his mouth. Nothing else matters when I am there. He looks at me with true love in his eyes, and his entire body language says, "Take me, I'm yours!" (Although I have caught the little devil red-handed on public TV exhibiting the same behavior to a gorgeous female reporter who came to do a segment on Frisky's.) Willie will make a slightly different high-pitched stress squeal when Johnny, a weeper capuchin in the neighboring enclosure, is taunting him with something Willie can't reach. Then there are sounds they make when they're hungry.

Willie

According to the Simian Society of America:

> Much of primate communication consists of a variety of vocalizations and facial expressions. When a Capuchin has lost sight of a companion, he or she may call out "Arahh-Arahh-Arahh" in an attempt to relocate the individual or its group. While feeding, "Uhm" is often heard throughout the entire session, especially when a particular food is enjoyed. Aggression is indicated by an open mouth threat while "Eh-Eh" is emitted. This is often heard while the monkey is lunging in a forward motion or slapping the ground and twitching the tail. A more pleasant sound is the low, quiet "Um-Um" or "groom me" vocalization which is heard in more rapid succession. (p. 53)

In short, it doesn't take long to understand the body language and sounds of monkeys. Although studies are still being done on the complexity of nonhuman primate communication, we seem to understand each other with what we know now.

Human communication, however, can be quite a bit more complicated—even if we speak the same language. In the business world, much of the daily communication now happens through e-mail and conference calls, eliminating our ability to read facial expressions and body language. The perils of that is the subject of Chapter 21, "Both-And."

In conference calls, as in so much other corporate communication, people often try to impress with business lingo. How many times have we all heard these terms, and others like them: synergy, strategic fit, leveraging assets, gap analysis, results-driven, ballpark, game plan ... the list goes on. I was recently e-mailed a brilliant game to play while on a conference call. It's called "Bull Bingo," and it was developed by Theodore R. Marmor from the Yale School of Management. The game is simple. It's played with a bingo card that has buzzwords like the ones just listed instead of numbers. When you hear one of the terms being used, you cross off or mark the spot. When you get five in a row, you stand up and shout "Bull!" What fun! I can hardly wait for my next conference call now! (I don't think I would ever *really* do this—but who knows?)

I thoroughly enjoyed listening to an audiobook called *Why Business People Speak Like Idiots: A Bullfighter's Guide*, by Brian Fugere, Chelsea Hardaway, and Jon Warshawsky. Some of the authors' points had me laughing out loud, because I could see that I was guilty of using some of the lingo they were making fun of. The authors define jargon as "using big words to make small points OR using big words to make no point at all ... Must we wear knee-high rubber boots to work to wade through the bull?" Their recommendation: "Kick the jargon habit. Make a point that is starkly clear."

So the next time you find yourself about to say something like, "Let's initiate an action plan," simply say instead, "Let's get started."

As for me, I'm off to Frisky's to see Willie—we understand each other.

Weekly Practice

Practice concise and clear speaking and writing. Make your point in simple language. In ten words or less, what is your company's mission?

Selected Resources

Fugere, Brian, Chelsea Hardaway, and Jon Warshawsky. *Why Business People Speak Like Idiots: A Bullfighter's Guide.* New York: Free Press, 2005.

Marmor, Theodore R., *Bull Bingo,* Yale School of Management, "FADS in MEDICAL CARE POLICY and POLITICS: New Ideas of Misleading Nostrums?" Accessed online 10/30/11 at www.pictureit.co.il/.../Media/.../Marmor.pps

Kirsch, Irwin S., Ann Jungeblut, Lynn Jenkins, and Andrew Kolstad. *Adult Literacy in America: A First Look at the Findings of the National Adult Literacy Survey,* NCES 1993-275. Washington, DC: US Government Printing Office, 2002.

Simian Society of America, The. *The Primate Care Handbook.* 2nd edition. Published by The Simian Society of America, Conway, AZ, 1997.

Part 5: Evolving Our Business Paradigm

Certitudes

Belief is the death of intelligence. As soon as one believes a doctrine of any sort, or assumes certitude, one stops thinking about that aspect of existence.

—Robert Anton Wilson

No mealworm is safe in the presence of a monkey. It is one of their favorite snack foods, packed full of protein and fat. That is, unless that monkey is Mr. Bojangles, a Java macaque. He used to make pets out of them. While the others devoured their mealworms without even a moment's pause to give thanks, Mr. Bojangles would lovingly "hoo hoo" over them, just as King Kong did with the lovely Ann Darrow in the 1933 film with Fay Wray (Naomi Watts played the part in the 2005 remake). In the movie, Kong fell in love with the lovely young actress and made a pet out of her. Mr. Bojangles seemed to want to do the same with his mealworms. If one of them fell off the shelf, he would carefully scoop it up and return it to safety, where he could protect it.

Mr. Bojangles

But wait a minute. Monkeys eat mealworms—right? Let's try again Maybe he was just full? But the results were the same every time—he never ate them.

Mr. Bojangles' behavior tests a "cherished certitude"—something we do or believe without question. Our personal cherished certitudes come from the influences of culture and/or religion and persist in our lives as behaviors and attitudes based on things we assume to be true. We are most often unaware that we are doing or thinking these things, because we're on "autopilot." It's usually not until we get hit on the head with the proverbial cosmic two by four that we even become aware of them. Mr. Bojangles' unusual behavior was an invitation to take a new look at one of these old assumptions.

I remember falling in love with a ring I had tried on at a women's expo. I had taken off my wedding ring to try it on and was admiring how beautiful it looked with my watch. My internal comment was, "What a shame I can't wear this ring on my wedding ring finger so that I can admire how beautiful it looks with my watch." It was then that my own cosmic two-by-four came out of nowhere and struck me in the head. I might have laughed out loud at myself; I'm not sure. In any event, I do remember the thought that made me laugh: it was the realization that I had been operating under the assumption that my wedding ring *had* to be worn on the left ring finger. Who made that up anyway? Then I was struck once more: "Wait a minute; I don't have to wear my watch on the left wrist either!" I always had, without questioning it. But why not wear it on the right wrist?

As the quote that opens this chapter advises, suspect all certitudes and question your convictions. Beliefs that are too tightly held can strangle the mind.

Bob Duggan, president of the Tai Sophia Institute for the Healing Arts, challenges his students to notice their certitudes. After all, science is continually unsettling old assumptions. He says to his graduate students, "I will feel my work is done if, when you graduate, you know absolutely nothing for certain."

And what about the many negative effects of certitudes in the workplace? Releasing certitudes and opening to new ways of handling familiar tasks and work practices can make room for innovation and creativity, evolving the whole business and moving it forward. For example, while most top restaurants claim to provide excellent service, at Ed Debevic's in Chicago, a tongue-in-cheek take on a 1950s diner in River North, the gum-snapping staff is part of the attraction. They're famous for serving up insults and wisecracks along with the burgers, shakes, and salads—not to mention jumping up on the counters to boogie along to piped-in music. Who would have thought going out to dinner for insults would be a success?

Then there's the Pike Place Fish Market, founded in 1930, located in Seattle, Washington. It is known for the tradition of fishmongers throwing the fish that a customer has purchased before it is wrapped. After nearing bankruptcy in 1986, the fish market owner and employees decided to become "world famous," changing their way of doing business by introducing their flying fish, games, and customer performances. Isn't throwing your food rude? Who would have guessed that throwing your food around could make you a world-famous destination with nearly ten thousand daily visitors?

These companies have challenged the certitudes of excellent restaurant service and fish market etiquette and have become successful because they did so.

I never met Mr. Bojangles. He had left the physical realm before I came to Frisky's Sanctuary. Even so, his life was a wake-up call. His gift is to remind us to continually check in on our convictions. A line from Shakespeare's *Hamlet* extends another invitation to check our certitudes—try substituting your own name for Horatio's.

> "There are more things in heaven and earth, Horatio,
> Than are dreamt of in your philosophy."

Weekly Practice

> *Question your certitudes in the workplace. Do you have certitudes around advertising? The number of days you must work? The way a certain task must be done? Take a look at your company policies with your coworkers and discuss how much of it is based on certitudes and assumptions.*

Selected Resources

Ed Debevic's, Chicago, IL. http://www.familyvacationcritic.com/chicago-restaurants/drt/

"Pike Place Fish Market." Wikipedia, accessed on line 3/10/11 http://en.wikipedia.org/wiki/Pike_Place_Fish_Market

Enough

Abundance is not something we acquire.
It is something we tune into."

—Wayne Dyer

At the sanctuary, we make a large bowl of fresh popcorn each day. This is used as a healthy, low-calorie snack for the monkeys. We also use it to distract the capuchins when they get to teasing one another and squealing too loudly—something that tends to happen at least once a day. (Monkeys are smart—methinks they could be staging this?)

Johnny, a twelve and a half pound male weeper capuchin, uses a surefire plan to get Willie, an older male, to start squealing—a high-pitched sound that capuchins make when they are alarmed or stressed out (or being mercilessly teased). With his arm extended as far as possible through the bars of his enclosure, Johnny waves a nice, soft piece of fleece bedding at Willie in the neighboring enclosure. The look on Johnny's face says, "Come on, Willie, you want this? You *know* you

Johnny

want this. Trust me; I won't pull it away this time!" And of course as Willie goes to grab it, Johnny pulls it away. Willie falls for it every time! (Come on, you know you did this to your little brother or cousin!)

So when I heard the squealing one day, I stopped what I was working on and grabbed the bowl of popcorn. Always two steps behind the monkeys, I held the entire bowl up to Johnny. I was operating on the honor system, figuring each monkey would take just one handful. But Johnny grabbed the bowl with one hand and used his entire free arm as a scoop to get out as much popcorn as he could! I said, "Hey, you little ... now there won't be enough for everyone else!" As if he cared!

Willie

That day, I found myself thinking in terms of *lack*. We tend to do this in business as well, believing that anyone else doing the same kind of work we do might take away all our business. In an interview that appeared in *The Hindu Business Line*, CEO Arun Agarwal of Cholamandalam MS General Insurance was asked if he was worried about being the "last player" to come into the general insurance industry. Did he see this as a disadvantage to his company? After all, there were companies out there that he could have approached that were now already insured by those who entered the industry earlier. Mr. Agarwal offers us another possibility in his response:

> It hasn't hurt us. On the contrary, it has helped us. We prepared our business plans, our systems and our products, after taking into account the collective experience of both the public and the private sector entrants. The market is big enough for everyone.

In another example, David Owen Ritz, who teaches an advanced course in prosperity-consciousness building, speaks to the power of moving beyond lack-mentality. In his course manual, *The Keys to the Kingdom*, Ritz writes:

> Your beliefs about your own highest potential are among the most important in determining how much prosperity and abundance you allow into your life. They are like the paper on which your inner road map is printed. Naturally you will find it difficult to move beyond the limitations placed on your life by your own beliefs, just as you would have trouble navigating beyond the edges of a road map. You cannot easily venture into territory that you do not know exists. These fundamental beliefs hold within themselves the key to all your personal possibilities and life potentials. They can either bind you or set you free. (p. 27)

The only lack that exists is the lack you *believe* in. Negative belief is what blocks unlimited good from flowing into our lives and our businesses. By eliminating your belief in lack, you prevent lack from showing up in your life. Suddenly, there is enough. When our sources of good are unlimited, the market is big enough for everyone.

I like what clothing designer Oluyinka Alawode has to say: "A business person should not feel threatened by bigger players; there is room for everyone. The sky is big enough for every bird to flap its wings and soar."

Johnny knows there is no lack of popcorn in the universe. Besides, I almost forgot—we have forty more bags in the kitchen.

Weekly Practice

> *Identify areas where you may be thinking in terms of lack. Universal law will attract that consciousness and make it appear to be true. For example, "We/I don't have enough money," "So and so got the promotion, so now there is nothing left for me," etc. Practice speaking only in terms of what you want to have and not what you*

are lacking. Practice a consciousness of "There is no lack in the universe." Notice what shows up when you banish lack thinking from your words and thoughts.

Selected Resources

Interview with CEO Arun Agarwal of Cholamandalam MS General Insurance. Article accessed online at *The Hindu Business Line* www.thehindubusinessline.com.

Alawode, Oluyinka. Accessed online at www.businessdayonline.com.

Ritz, David Owen. *The Keys to the Kingdom workbook, 2002.* P. 27, www.newthoughtsforliving.com

Security

Change is inevitable—except from a vending machine.

—Robert C. Gallagher

I know you've heard the old saying, "The only constant in life is change." Why, then, do we sometimes feel stuck? The truth is, we are never really stuck. Life is in constant motion. Even when we feel stuck, we're in motion. We may just be spinning in place.

After the death of Sam, Jackie's beloved companion of twenty-two years, Jackie had to adjust to life without him. At the sanctuary, we took many steps to persuade Jackie, a twenty-three-year-old vervet guenon monkey, to share an indoor/outdoor enclosure with Angel, a much younger mona guenon monkey.

Jackie

This didn't happen overnight. Just imagine losing your life partner on Tuesday, and on Wednesday, a new one moves in. It's not likely that would go over well—and humans tend not to bite!

Jackie went into a sort of withdrawal. She ended up spending most of her time indoors with her stuffed toys, her babies, even though she now had the option to go outside whenever she wanted. Angel (don't let the name fool you) also loved Jackie's babies. Instead of nurturing and grooming them, however, Angel would rip them to shreds. Passive little Jackie sadly sat back and let it happen.

More than a year passed, and then we noticed a change—a role reversal. Jackie began to fight back. She would no longer allow Angel to take her toys and rip them to shreds. Jackie began standing up for herself, and Angel retreated.

Change is a constant in the work environment as well. "Job security" is an ideal that we cling to, yet when we look back through thousands of years of history, it becomes clear that job security is a relatively new concept, one that is also in motion.

Currently, the average time an individual spends in one job is only four to six years. People are even changing careers two or three times in their lifetimes, rather than sticking with one job or career. So now we must learn the necessary skills to manage life's changes.

In an article entitled "Leading the Workplace Within," author Ida Covi writes, "Refocus job loyalty to being loyal to yourself. Don't be complacent. Keep your skills and resume fresh and stay on top of what the hot trends are. Ask yourself how you fit into them."

In the book *What Would Buddha Do At Work? 101 Answers to Workplace Dilemmas*, authors Metcalf and Hateley are clear that job security has been an illusion all along. "Our only job security is our ability to secure a job. Work with that." (p. 133)

Downsizings and layoffs are part of business reality. Knowing that an employer is not obligated to keep you forever gives you the chance to choose to keep yourself employable. This is a practice that will help to evolve not only your own business life but the business community as a whole.

Ultimately, you have control over your own life. You can choose to release your insecurities and adopt the following as a part of both your resumé and your work ethic: "navigates smoothly through change." Be strong in your convictions. Take all the training you can, and continue to update your skills.

Jackie is standing up for herself, reminding me that it does not serve me to play victim, or to continue telling the story, "I have no other choice." So off I go to freshen up my skills.

Weekly Practice

> *Learn something new. Go to a conference or sign up for a class. Even something that doesn't seem related could bring new insights.*

Selected Resources

Covi, Ida. *Leading the Workplace Within.* Article accessed online at http://www.businessknowhow.com/manage/leadwithin.htm

Metcalf, Franz and B. J. Gallagher Hateley. *What Would Buddha Do at Work? 101 Answers to Workplace Dilemmas.* P. 133. Berkeley, CA: Ulysses Press; and San Francisco: Berrett-Koehler Publishers, 2001.

One Thing

Dress me slowly, for I am in a great rush.

—Napoleon Bonaparte

This day was about like any other at Frisky's. As a wildlife rehabilitator and caregiver to twenty-three primates who were former pets, Colleen was rushing around, filling water bottles, and passing out fruit. She had a couple of volunteers stuffing envelopes for her on the front porch for an upcoming mailing. Spring and summer are particularly busy seasons for a wildlife rehabilitator because of the number of motherless baby rabbits, squirrels, and birds that come in daily. It would not be unusual to take in fourteen babies in a single day. Often they are so young that they still need bowel and bladder encouragement, which is usually the job of the mother.

Babee

Colleen's able and quick hands were moving at record pace to replace Babee's water bottle. Babee, a twelve-year-old female weeper capuchin monkey weighing 9.5 pounds, was even quicker. Wanting Colleen to slow down and visit with her a while, she reached out and grabbed hold of the spaghetti strap on the summer top Colleen was wearing. As Colleen pulled away in surprise, Babee pulled harder on the strap; within seconds, Babee was holding the entire shredded top inside of her enclosure and was looking quite pleased with her accomplishment.

Now Colleen is one of the most selfless, hardworking, and giving people I know—but never had I actually seen her "give the shirt off her back."

As the stars, the moon, and the sun would have it at that moment, a car pulled up to drop off some donations. All that was between Colleen and the generous person on the other side of the fence were some privacy slats, but if one really wanted to peek in, there were some definite gaps to do so. Colleen grabbed two paper towels that were within reach and yelled, "I'll be there in a moment!"

Reflecting on this event and expecting some sympathy from me, she realized the lesson Babee had taught her. Rushing often ends up slowing us down in the end. What Colleen did not know was that I had asked the universe for a good laugh that day!

Like most people, even if I am only doing one thing, my mind often races ahead to what I have to do next. I do not think Colleen and I are the only ones who try to do several things at once. Thich Nhat Hanh, in his book *Peace Is Every Step,* offers daily mindfulness practices to help us learn to be fully present in all that we do. Here is one way that he offers the practice of mindfulness:

> If I am incapable of washing dishes joyfully, if I want to finish them quickly so that I can go have dessert, I will not feel the warmth of the water on my hands or each movement of my hands. And I will be equally incapable of enjoying my dessert. With fork in hand, I will be thinking about what to do next, and the texture and the flavor of the dessert, together with the pleasure of eating it, will be lost. I will always be dragged into the future, never able to live in the present moment. (p. 26)

I once had to journal about the practice of Doing One Thing at a Time for a class on stillness at the Tai Sophia Institute. At first it was extremely painful. I caught myself doing things like eating breakfast and writing my "to do" list at the same time. Oops, that's two things! By the end of a couple of days of allowing myself to do just one thing at a time, I noticed not only that I was still accomplishing everything that needed to be done, but that I felt much less overwhelmed as well.

So try this at work, where it has likely become an accepted practice (or maybe even an expected one) to "multitask." Do not answer or read e-mail while you are on hold on the phone. Notice your breathing instead. Do not make copies while making coffee and do not stuff envelopes while sitting in a meeting. Do not eat lunch while working on a report. In our multitasking culture, it's also become common practice even to answer a cell phone call or to send and receive text messages while in conversation with another person. Do not text or answer your cell phone while in a meeting.

If we set an intention to cease this multitasking, we can learn, with practice, to be fully present in each thing we do. The first couple of days can be tough, but once you get through that, you can start to relax into it, or because of it! Our work and our relationships will be the richer for it.

And if you are still having a hard time, we will let you replace Babee's water bottle.

Weekly Practice

> *For one week, do only one thing at a time. Notice the resistance or nonresistance of this practice. Does it change during the course of the week?*

Selected Resources

Hanh, Thich Nhat. *Peace is Every Step: The Path of Mindfulness in Everyday Life.* P. 26, New York: Bantam Books, 1991.

Ring-Around-the-Rosy

If you want to build a ship, don't drum up people together to collect wood and don't assign them tasks and work, but rather teach them to long for the endless immensity of the sea.

—Antoine de Saint-Exupery

I was completely surprised by her strength. Bimbee, a weeper capuchin monkey, was thirty-five years old and weighed only 8.4 pounds, so I figured I could take her easily if I had to. I had played the tug-of-war game with her bigger roommates and won. When I checked the records for her weight, I found that although she appeared smaller than her roommates, Oogie and Isadora, she actually weighed more than they do. I think Oogie and Isadora were being easy on me and simply enjoyed the motion of the tugging back and forth. Bimbee was different—she wanted the taste of victory.

Bimbee

Margaret J. Wheatley's fascinating book, *Leadership and the New Science,* describes how today's businesses are built on the philosophical underpinnings of an outdated world. Wheatley contends that that outdated world view needs to be made current in order to bring our business culture into congruence with other areas of public life:

> Each of us lives and works in organizations designed from seventeenth-century physics, from Newtonian mechanics. It is the basis from which we design and manage organizations and from which we do research in all of the social sciences. Intentionally or not, we work from a world view that is strongly anchored in the natural sciences. But the science has changed.
>
> If we are to continue to draw from science to create and manage organizations, to design research, and to formulate ideas about organizational design and human motivation, then we need to at least ground our work in the science of our times. The new physics explains there are no recipes or formulas, no checklist or expert advice that describes "reality." If context is as crucial as the science explains, nothing really transfers; everything is always new and different and unique to each of us. We must engage with each other. (p. 7–9)

Today's businesses are based on the organizational structure of a pyramid, as is evident from the visual structure of most organizational charts. A pyramid has a definite hierarchy. In a big organization, it is not uncommon for the person at the top of the pyramid to interact very little, or not at all, with the people at the bottom. This can leave employees feeling disconnected and disengaged—with a sense that their opinions don't matter. Mike Moore's "Motivational Plus" newsletter features a story that illustrates this peril of the pyramid:

> It seems that a rather prestigious country club was having a problem with disappearing bottles of shampoo in the men's shower room. No matter what the management did, the bottles kept disappearing. Signs were posted and meetings were held encouraging the members to leave the shampoo bottles where they found them. Nothing worked.

> One day the manager of the club was inspecting the shower room while a custodian was mopping the floor. When the manager saw that another shampoo bottle had disappeared, he expressed his anger and frustration to the custodian.
>
> "We've tried everything. Nothing works. What more can we do?" The custodian stopped mopping, looked up at the manager and said, "Why don't you take the top off each new bottle of shampoo and throw it away? Nobody will take a shampoo bottle without a top." When the manager asked him why he hadn't offered this great solution before, the custodian replied, "Nobody ever asks my opinion, so nobody gets my opinion."

Imagine if the prevailing organizational structure were a circle instead. In a circular structure, everyone would be involved in the planning, and everyone would have a say. Each worker would have a more vested interest in the business's outcomes if they had a voice in helping to make the decisions.

Wheatley paints a picture of what is needed as we evolve our current business practices toward a vision of shared leadership:

> In this chaotic world, we need leaders. But we don't need bosses. We need leaders to help us develop the clear identity that lights the dark moments of confusion. We need leaders to support us as we learn how to live by our values. We need leaders who understand that we are best controlled by concepts that invite our participation, not policies and procedures that curtail our contribution. And people need to be able to reach past traditional boundaries and develop relationships with people anywhere in the system. (p. 146)

Today's business practices can sometimes seem like a tug-of-war, with one "side" always trying to beat the other—a winner who defeats a loser. If we approach our work from the mind-set of competition, the results we create will reflect our assumptions. In my game of tug-of-war with Bimbee, before I actually reached out to her, I assumed that because she appeared smaller than her roommates, she couldn't offer me a competitive game. But when I actually engaged with her, I found out differently—and now I have a new respect for her strength. I think the two of us could even take on Isadora and Oogie head-to-head.

But I'd rather include them and play ring-around-the-rosy instead.

Weekly Practice

> *Have each department write down an issue or challenge that they have been struggling with. Exchange issues with another department and, as a department team, come up with a possible solution or suggestion for the other department. Include everyone on the payroll. Have everyone in the room at the same time to make their offerings. Each team should accept the suggestion with grace. No telling the others "why it wouldn't work." Just observe it for a while before you decide if it is feasible.*

Selected Resources

Moore, Mike. "Motivational Plus" newsletter. www.motivationalplus.com

Wheatley, Margaret J. *Leadership and the New Science.* San Francisco: Berrett-Koehler Publishers, 1999.

Flow

Every one of our greatest national treasures,
our liberty, enterprise, vitality, wealth, military power, global authority,
flow from a surprising source: our ability to give thanks.

—Tony Snow

Running water is too often taken for granted. I rarely think about it as a luxury. The truth is, I rarely think about it at all—I just expect it to flow from the faucet when I turn the tap. My awareness and gratitude around the flow of clean drinking water increased because of daily reminders coming my way. The Prenter Water Fund came together in the summer of 2008 a few months after residents of Prenter Hollow found out that the groundwater they had used and depended on for generations had been contaminated by coal slurry injections due to mountaintop removal. With high illness rates occurring, and a lack of government willingness to help, the residents set up the Prenter Water Fund as a way to reach out for our support in obtaining clean drinking water.

My little cat, Spooky, is completely fascinated with the flow of running water. I often find her sitting on the ledge of the bathroom sink, looking up the mouth of the faucet. Whenever I turn on the faucet lately, she is right there to investigate. She is so close to the flow that I have to remove her so that I can get to it.

One of the tasks that is Colleen's responsibility as manager of Frisky's Sanctuary is to make sure that all the animals have abundant fresh water. For its residents, the sanctuary uses the kind of water bottle with a metal spout that angles out from the bottle's bottom. The spout itself has a small, freely moving metal ball at the lower end that gravity holds in place, blocking the opening and keeping the water inside. The water only flows when the animal pushes up on the ball with its tongue.

One day, after removing an empty water bottle from the enclosure shared by Darrow and Darwin, two gothic squirrel monkeys, Colleen told me, "Darrow and Darwin have figured out how to get running water. They stick little bits of vegetables from their dinner up the spout of the bottle to hold it open, and the water runs right out. They use it to wash their hands, and they like to watch it flow. I'm always having to refill their water and clean out the bits of food they've jammed up there." Now, these monkeys are not even in sight of a sink where they could have observed the flow of water and the human practice of hand-washing. How very clever they are!

Darrow and Darwin

All these situations coming my way that have to do with healthy water flow remind me that I need to pay more attention to flow in my own life—in more ways than one. At the time of writing this chapter, the news has been full of messages about the stagnant economy. Money is not flowing. Another word for money is "currency," which comes from the Latin word *currere*, meaning "to run" or "to flow." In *The Seven Spiritual Laws of Success*, author Deepak Chopra writes:

> If we stop the circulation of money, if it is our only intention to hold on to it and hoard it, since it is life energy, we will stop its circulation back into our lives as well. In order to keep that energy coming to us, we have to keep the energy circulating. Like a river,

> money must keep flowing, otherwise it begins to stagnate, to clog, to suffocate, and strangle its very own life force.(p. 28–29)

Is it possible to keep business thriving and flowing when we are constantly bombarded with news of the opposite? Yes, it is. As I was researching key actions that keep business flowing and even growing in a recession, two things that kept showing up were gratitude and appreciation. It turns out that the simple act of sending a handwritten thank-you note has a profound effect on business growth.

Vanessa Lowry, a connection expert and owner of Profits in Progress, helps businesses incorporate the dynamic tool of handwritten notes into their marketing strategies and connections solutions:

> The most successful sales professionals are masters at building relationships with the contacts they make. Handwritten notes are highly effective in getting a sales professional in the door for a cold contact. This story from Robert Middleton's "The More Clients Blog" illustrates the impact of a handwritten note with a 90% effectiveness rate:
>
> "One of my clients carefully selected a list of 20 HR directors and sent them a series of 4 articles; each mailing was personalized with a handwritten note. His final mailing was a letter asking for an appointment.
>
> "In his follow-up calls he was able to get 18 appointments. That's a 90% success rate! My client pointed out that he wasn't trying to sell, but establish credibility and develop relationships. Several of these connections ultimately turned into clients [for him]."

P. Scanlon, fitness, image, and lifestyle consultant and president of Roswell Healthy Lifestyle Advisory Board, reports:

> I truly believe that sending a note to someone distinguishes a level of customer service. One month alone, sending personal

> notes increased my business by 87%! And I've seen the value in the way people respond to me once they've received my thoughtful note.

Kody Bateman, the founder of SendOutCards, says, "Appreciation wins out over self-promotion every time." Kody has set up a system which makes writing a note much simpler and less time consuming.

In business, writing a personal note isn't about sending someone a card with your logo on it as an advertisement. Blatant self-promotion is not necessary. All you need to say is something like, "I enjoyed meeting you at the networking event the other day," mentioning specifically the name of the event and the date, and another line or two to personalize the note. To make this practice easy and convenient, keep some blank note cards, thank-you cards, and stamps handy, and write a couple each week. Then notice what happens in your business.

Gratitude is simple, yet it has so much power. Gratitude and appreciation not only keep positive energy flowing but also keep our business practices evolving in a more positively focused way. You will also find that there is a connection between the flow of gratitude and the flow of money. Keeping money circulating is important as well. All it takes to start seeing a difference is to circulate just a little bit more money and gratitude than you are circulating now.

Remember, all it took for Darrow and Darwin to go from having water that didn't flow to water that did was a couple tiny morsels of food.

Weekly Practice

> *Practice gratitude. Write thank-you notes. Observe if there has been any increase in the flow of good into your life.*

Selected Resources

Chopra, Deepak. *The Seven Spiritual Laws of Success.* Amber-Allen Publishing and New World Library, San Rafael, CA, 1994.

Lowry, Vanessa. *The Power of Appreciation Handwritten Notes Can Increase Influence and Trust.* Article accessed online at www.training-modules.com/contributions/appreciation.asp, 4/14/11

Bateman, Cody. Accessed online 7/23/10 at www.sendoutcards.com

Associates

I like pigs. Dogs look up to us. Cats look down on us.
Pigs treat us as equals.

—Winston Churchill

It's time for CoCo's insulin shot. He can see his caregiver, Colleen, enter the macaque house, where he is housed with four other monkeys. Each has his or her own separate enclosure. Without any words or pleas from Colleen, CoCo willingly comes to the edge of his pen and places his rear against the gate. Colleen administers the shot of insulin, and CoCo turns around to receive the healthy treat that he can expect, without exception.

This routine takes place twice each and every day at Frisky's. So as not to cause any disputes, upsets, or hurt feelings among CoCo's roommates, they all receive a treat, too. Trying to explain to them that CoCo got a snack because of his diabetes would be about as easy as explaining to a two-year-old why his friend got an ice cream cone but he didn't—neither has developed the ability to reason logically or

CoCo

control emotions. With the exception of the insulin shot, no primate in this house receives any special treatment over another. Each one has been honored with a treat, so each one feels just as respected and important as all the others. Ahhh, contentment in the macaque house!

Such equality of treatment is not the norm in today's corporate environment. However, corporations do exist where evolved business practices set the standard for the rest of the business world. Gore Associates in Newark, Delaware, is one such company.

Gore Associates, a privately held, multimillion-dollar high-tech firm, makes the water-resistant fabric known as Gore-Tex, among many other products. This company has chosen not to use job titles to distinguish between one position and other. No one outside the company knows who holds which position. In *The Tipping Point,* author Malcolm Gladwell writes about his visit to this company. He says that if you ask employees of Gore Associates for their business cards, each card simply lists the employee's name and the same word next to it—"Associate." This is *regardless* of the employee's salary or level of responsibility. At Gore, people don't have bosses; they have sponsors or mentors, who watch out for their interests. There are no organizational charts, budgets, or elaborate strategic plans. All of the offices look the same. There are no "executive suites" that promote the aura of rank or upgraded position. Gore Associates also keeps its facilities small. When the parking lot becomes full, they simply build another plant. Whenever business experts make lists of "The Best American Companies to Work For," Gore Associates is on the list.

Take a moment to consider which is more important: that you talk to someone with an impressive title, or you talk to someone who is going to get the job done? Would you be more impressed by a Vision Clearance Executive (window washer) or a Field Nourishment Officer (waitress)? Do you remember people's titles, or do you remember the work they did for you?

CoCo and his primate pals could be giving corporate America a hint. Treat *everyone* as special, and there will be fewer breakdowns and conflicts in the house. Things will run more smoothly overall, and everyone will feel respected. Although it's true that CoCo gets the shot in the rear a couple of times a day from Colleen, the others don't seem to mind that they miss that part. Perhaps they know that because of CoCo, they all get treats, and they are all Associates.

Weekly Practice

Consider titles and all constructs by asking the following questions:

Where is it of use?

Where is it a noose?

What does it reveal?

What does it conceal?

(From John G. Sullivan, "The Wave and Particle Song," *Five Chants from John to You* (handout), Laurel, MD, Tai Sophia Institute, 2004.

Selected Resources

Malcolm Gladwell. *The Tipping Point*. New York: Little, Brown, 2000.

Part 6:
Opening to Optimism

Smile

Scatter joy.

—Ralph Waldo Emerson

Nothing starts the work day off better than being greeted with a smile and the simple words, "Good morning!" It is a beautiful gift to receive. If you've ever worked in an environment where such courtesies are missing, then you know what I mean. That acknowledgment and that smile say, "I notice you—this is a worthwhile interaction." The simple act of turning up the corners of your mouth creates an instant connection between you and someone else.

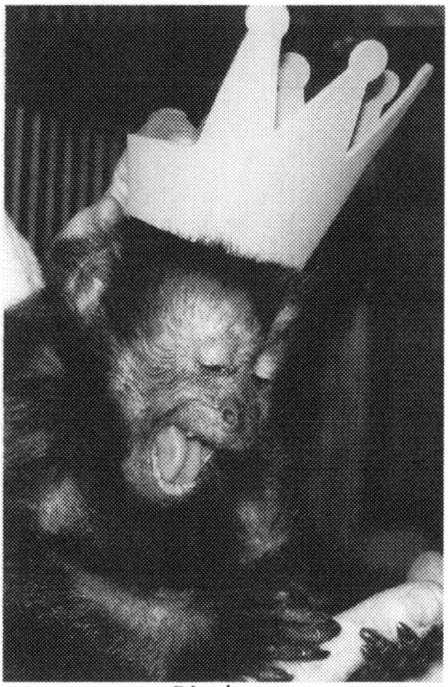

Bimbee

When I greet Bimbee, a female weeper capuchin monkey, with a smile on my face and say, "hello Bimbee!" what I get in return just melts my heart. I know my heart is melting because I get a warm sensation and "liquid heart" starts to form in my eyes, often rolling down my cheeks. I have heard it said that when the heart is full, the eyes overflow. Bimbee comes to greet me at the edge of her enclosure with glistening eyes and a smile from ear to ear. She rubs her belly at the same time as if to say, "This is delicious! You are noticing and acknowledging me. I feel so special. *You* are special." Bimbee is a reminder that we all crave acknowledgment.

In the corporate training video *Smile*, Seattle bus driver Reggie Wilson transforms a dreary bus ride into an experience his customers look forward to. Reggie tells jokes in which he asks for passengers' participation, and he also sings to the people on his bus. There are people who specifically wait for Reggie's bus, letting other buses pass them by. He doesn't always feel like smiling, but for the sake of his customers, he makes the *choice* to smile. In the process, he feels better too. This real life story of Reggie Wilson and the difference he makes to people is now told in this training video about exceptional customer service.

Dianne Connelly of the Tai Sophia Institute reminds us that even our simplest daily choices have the power to open our minds to an optimistic way of being in the world. In her book *Medicine Words: Language of Love for the Treatment Room of Life*, Connelly writes about how language is a kind of medicine, in the same sense that many Native American tribes use the word "medicine." Woodland Indians such as the Cherokee and Iroquois carried medicine pouches that held not only plants with medicinal properties but also personal items and good luck charms. Connelly writes, "*Smile* is a medicine word. It belongs in our medicine pouch as a daily practice, as a gift, as a way of life." (p. 104) She reminds us that our words and practices create heaven or hell with each thing we say and do.

Your enthusiasm and your smile will stay in your clients' memories, creating business referrals. You can choose to be the person your client looks forward to hearing from. When you're on the phone, put a smile on your face—it will come through the phone in your tone of voice. Practice smiling at the people you pass on the street or in the hallways at work, and notice how life shows up differently for you. All kinds of opportunities and interactions will come your way that didn't before.

In a study of more than a thousand people, Harris Interactive found that 94 percent of the respondents said they are likely to notice a person's smile before they notice the person's height or appearance. And 75 percent of the respondents felt that an attractive smile is important for success in the workplace. So, perhaps it is not necessary to wear a $1,200 suit to work every day—a smile really is your best accessory, giving you an instant facelift to boot.

And besides that, Bimbee doesn't care what I am wearing!

Weekly Practice

Smile at everyone. There is a ripple effect. Observe the benefits.

Selected Resources

Connelly, Dianne. *Medicine Words: Language of Love for the Treatment Room of Life.* P. 104, Tai Sophia Press, 2009, Laurel, MD

Osteryoung, Jerry. "A Simple Smile is Good For Business." Accessed online 3/19/11 at http://jmi. fsu.edu/Services/Jerry-s-Articles/The-Heart-and-Soul-of-Your-Business/ASimple-Smile-Is-Good-for-Business

Smile. A corporate training video produced by Joel Lesko. A product of SunShower Learning, www.smile-video.com

The Key

Man is made or unmade by himself. By the right choice he ascends. As a being of power, intelligence, and love, and the lord of his own thoughts, he holds the key to every situation.

—James Allen

Recently I was talking to the birds at Frisky's, who have become residents since their owners gave up on them. I like to let them know I care about them. They are very sensitive creatures, and they enjoy the one-on-one attention.

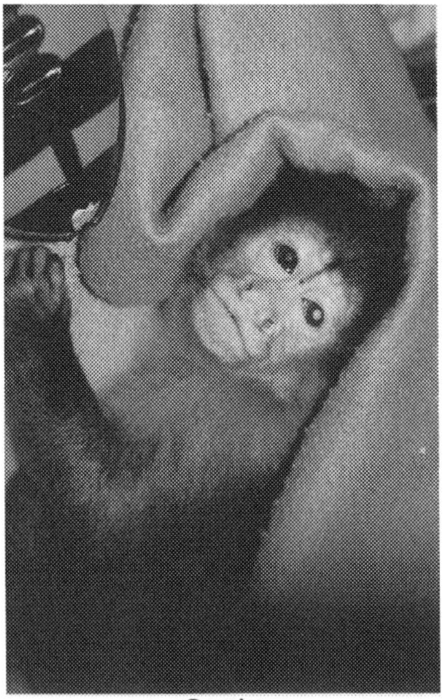

Oogie

But a noise distracted me. It sounded like someone had pulled up in the sanctuary's driveway and was beeping his horn. I looked out the window, but nobody was there. That's when I realized it was Oogie, a cinnamon capuchin monkey, playing with a motion-activated toy. She loves her toys and loves physical contact: hand-to-hand, tail-to-hand, feet-to-hand—it doesn't matter to her. (That's *her* feet and *my* hands, just in case you were picturing it the other way around.) Once she had my attention, she frantically started trying to fit her big new key chain with real keys on it through the bars of her enclosure.

"What are these keys for, Oogie?" I asked. Of course she couldn't answer me in words, but those keys nevertheless had unlocked the door to my attention, which is what Oogie wanted.

In his course *The Keys to the Kingdom,* David Owen Ritz teaches that our *consciousness* is the key to our prosperity. That is, our thoughts, our beliefs, and our words determine the amount of prosperity we allow into our lives. With all the recent media coverage of the recession, it is all too easy to let television, newspapers, and the Internet lead us into believing that the economy is doomed and we're all in a heap of trouble. When the collective consciousness believes that and speaks that, it becomes so—Ritz's point exactly.

Now, I am by no means an authority on finances and investments—I can't even get a handle on the language. But there are some gems of information that I have picked up from financial advisors such as David Slade of Edward Jones in Ellicott City, Maryland. David showed me a chart of historical events in the past hundred years and how they have affected the market. Historically, after major world events such as the terrorist attacks of September 11, 2001, the stock market takes a hit. Then, within a two- to three-year period, it returns to its previous level. History has borne this out again and again. In many cases, this rebound occurs even sooner.

The point is that the market *always* recovers. I believe the reason why it does is that people's fear subsides—and in turn, the market comes back up. Another financial advisor once told me that it is when his clients are the most afraid that he tries to increase his own personal investments. Quoting him, "When things look scary, write a check."

A post I once read on "The Daily Guru," an online source of inspirational and motivational quotations, had this to say about prosperity:

> What you will discover about abundance and prosperity is that it has nothing to do with opportunities, chance, luck, or even training, education, or skill. Your boss, the stock market, your job, interest rates, or the economy have nothing to do with your prosperity. You, and only you, control your prosperity. And you do so by the consciousness you develop. Once you get this awareness, the results start showing up immediately.

Donald Trump makes decisions using his gut instinct. He says he literally feels it in his gut when something is right. For example, in 1993, when the market was horrible and he owed just about every bank in New York City money, his gut told him to buy the building at 40 Wall Street. He made several offers to people to go in fifty-fifty with him on the purchase of the building. Nobody would take him up on it—they thought he was crazy. Regardless, he purchased it on his own for just over $1 million. Fourteen years later, he turned down an offer for $535 million for the same building. Since then, two of the people he'd approached to partner with him on the deal told him it was the worst deal they *never* made.

In the book *Spiritual Economics—The Principles and Process of True Prosperity*, author Eric Butterworth mentions an old *Wall Street Journal* article that stated, "Positive thinking is the way out of economic malaise" (116). The article went on to decry the excessive pessimism that is now engulfing us. It also quoted the president of a large corporation as urging business leaders to adopt a more positive attitude to help dispel fears of impending economic doom and to restore confidence in the American people.

Be constantly vigilant about what you think and speak. When you want to change something in your life, focus on what you *want*. Do not focus on the doom and gloom of what others are speaking or what appears to be reality at the moment. The market comes back up—it always has, and it always will. Butterworth offers this affirmation: "I accept the reality of this situation, but not its permanence." By nurturing a positive mind-set within ourselves, we help to create a more optimistic business environment overall.

When Oogie handed me her big new key chain, I think she was handing me the keys to my consciousness so that I could release any limiting and gloomy thoughts that I might have picked up from the morning news.

Weekly Practice:

> *Speak only in terms of what you want. Don't ever mention anything that isn't a thought of prosperity, abundance, and life moving forward. Notice the way you word things.*

Instead of:	*Use:*
Don't forget ...	*Remember to ...*
I can't afford that ...	*I'm saving for ...*
I am always in debt ...	*I am working my way to financial freedom ...*
I can't do that ...	*I'm a beginner ...*
I'm too old ...	*I'm starting anew at ...*

Selected Resources

Butterworth, Eric. *Spiritual Economics: The Principles and Process of True Prosperity.* Unity Village, MO: Unity House, 1993.

Trump, Donald. *Think Big and Kick Ass—in Business and in Life*. New York: HarperCollins 2007.

"The Daily Guru." Accessed online at www.thedailyguru.com, February 26, 2004.

Bananas

If I have been of service, if I have glimpsed more of
the nature and essence of ultimate good,

if I am inspired to reach wider horizons of thought and action,

if I am at peace with myself, it has been a successful day.

—Alex Noble

Colleen was looking exhausted and sounding irritated. She had every right to be. Her husband, Scott, had been gone for weeks, helping to restore power to the victims of Hurricane Katrina—God bless him. At the time, Scott was a mechanic for Riggs Distler, a contractor for Baltimore Gas and Electric. Colleen knew that his absence was for a higher good. She never once complained about his being gone, even though it meant he wasn't there to help care for the more than one hundred animals at the sanctuary—sometimes with the help of volunteers, and sometimes not.

Yoo and Johnny

At this moment, Colleen had just come in the door from attending to some "squawks" that were coming from the outdoor capuchin monkey enclosures. She had already mentioned to me that Willie, Babee, Johnny, and Yoo (all weeper capuchins, with the exception of Willie, who is a wedge-capped capuchin) had been exhibiting "so much attitude lately" (Colleen's words). She and I discussed why that might be so. I asked if the monkeys might be picking up on her exhaustion and the nervous energy from all her rushing around. She said, "Maybe—but I think the real reason is that I haven't been able to go to the store to get them their bananas. That's one of their favorite daily snacks. Scott usually stops after work to pick them up."

Bananas contain an essential amino acid called *tryptophan*, which helps you to calm down and relax. Apples and turkey contain it as well. Between Scott's absence, the change in the monkeys' routine, and the missing stress-reducing nutrient from the bananas, it's no wonder that Colleen's work was more stressful than usual.

At times, everyone experiences workplace stress—it's part of doing business. But there are countless ways to make the stress more manageable, and numerous excellent resources for businesses that want to create a more optimistic work environment. For example, Bob Nelson's *1001 Ways to Reward Employees* offers fabulous ideas about how to make employees feel appreciated and how to create work environments that are pleasant and friendly. Here is a small sampling of suggestions from the book that involve tried-and-true practices from the companies that have put them in place:

- Reader's Digest sets aside space for employees to plant gardens. For a nominal cost, they will even plow and fertilize the land.
- Control Data Corporation in Minneapolis also has garden plots where employees can grow their own vegetables.
- Levi Strauss & Company, headquartered in San Francisco, has a quiet room where an employee can take a solitary break to relax, pound on the walls, scream, meditate, or read.

Many hospitals and other corporations are setting up "humor carts," or even dedicated physical rooms where people can read funny books, watch funny videos, or play with funny gadgets such as wind-up chattering teeth. Laughter in the workplace has been attributed to increased employee motivation, improved working relationships, and increased levels of creativity and productivity. Create an atmosphere of fun and you'll get great work! Companies are starting to recognize that laughter also relaxes muscles, eases tension, and even reduces pain. Laughter can be added to the list of management strategies to alleviate job dissatisfaction, stress, and absenteeism.

Formal studies are also starting to document the negative effects of workplace stress. For example, Gallup has conducted a twenty-five-year study of more than a million employees showing that an employee's length of employment and level of productivity are directly related to the quality of the manager and the environment that he or she creates. According to their study, people leave managers, not companies.

Some forward-thinking companies are offering stress-reducing services to their employees. My friend, Jackie Simmons, runs a business called Stress Management Services, in which she offers shiatsu to employees in the workplace. When a business contracts with her for her services, she brings a seated massage chair to the workplace and offers sessions to interested employees. During each private session, she applies pressure to specific points on the person's body to enhance muscle relaxation and reduce the negative effects of stress.

All of these measures are great ways to help create a healthier, more positively focused work environment. And perhaps the simplest and most cost-effective thing to do would be to follow the monkeys' lead and give every employee a banana each day.

Weekly Practice

> *Take one step toward creating a pleasant and friendly workplace, using an example from the chapter. Next week, take another step ...*

Selected Resources

Nelson, Bob, PhD. *1001 Ways to Reward Employees*. New York: Workman Publishing, 2005.

Gallup Organization study accessed online 11/10/11 at http://webcenters.netscape.compuserve.com/whatsnew/package.jsp?name=fte/quitjobs/quitjobs&floc=wn-dx

Buckingham, Marcus, and Curt Coffman. *First, Break All the Rules: What the World's Greatest Managers Do Differently.* New York: Simon & Schuster. 1999 copyright held by the Gallup Organization.

Favorite Places

You're on your own, and you know what you know.
And you will be the guy who'll decide where you'll go.
Oh, the places you'll go.

—Dr. Seuss

Dawson's space is the first enclosure a visitor sees when entering the macaque house at Frisky's Sanctuary. Colleen takes great care to ensure this enclosure makes a good first impression, just as we would in a foyer or reception area at work. She lays out Dawson's blankets and his pieces of fleece fabric "just so," and she even lines up his little toy trucks. But Dawson has a different idea about how his space should look. He wants to give it his *own* personal touch, so he totally rearranges everything that Colleen has neatly laid out—by throwing things all over the place.

Dawson

Dawson is a male Java macaque, born April 25, 2001. He came to Frisky's when he was five months old. After his human parents divorced, they could no longer keep him legally. Colleen called him her "cling-on," because he was a very clingy baby. He remained physically close to Colleen for about three years. It's at about age three that monkeys' "needy" behavior changes, becoming similar to that of human children as they enter their early teens. They have their own ideas about things, which often do not match their parents'.

This makes me think about how individual tastes differ and what brings comfort and joy to each of us as individuals. An example comes to mind from a group discussion I took part in soon after arriving back from one of my favorite places in the world, a tiny mountain town in northern Idaho called Clark Fork. It was in this town that my daughter attended her sophomore year of high school. With a population of only 550, the town is so small that the quip "Don't blink or you'll miss it" just about describes it. Yet if you spend two weeks there, you realize that Clark Fork contains the whole world. One woman in the discussion who heard my description said, "Oh, my God, that would drive me nuts! Give me New York City!"

In a study conducted by Kalevi Mikael Korpela, PhD, and Matti P. Yien, MPsych, at the University of Tampere in Finland, they found that spending time in favorite places alleviates stress but also helps regulate strong emotions. Members of one group were asked to visit their favorite local place five times during the week on average. The members of the other group were asked to visit their favorite local place only one time or not at all. Each group kept a journal about the places they visited outside the home during that week. The results state that the people from the group that visited favorite places several times per week experienced a stronger restorative experience than did the people from the group that did not visit their favorite places. "The conclusion is that 'favorite-place' prescriptions and visits affect subjective well-being. Health counseling and research on coping strategies should not ignore the use of sociophysical environments for self and emotion regulation." (pp. 435–438)

Now since many people only look forward to two days out of seven, wouldn't it be great if we could reverse those numbers? That way, on Sunday night we'd be saying, "Yahoo! Tomorrow's Monday—back to work, my favorite place!" Although this isn't likely to happen, there may be ways to make the transition from weekend to the beginning of the work week a little less painful. One of them is to take the Finnish researchers' advice and put it to work in your own life. I've come up with a list of ten characteristics of favorite places. Here's how you can tell when a place is one of *your* favorites:

1. There's no tension in your shoulders, or any other place where you usually feel tension or pain. (I made a recent visit to my own favorite place, and the daily tension I feel in my shoulders was gone for the whole five days I was there.)
2. You want to throw your arms up in the air and say, "Yes! I'm here! Thank you!"
3. A smile comes easily and effortlessly.
4. The place itself has sentimental value for you.
5. You see the extraordinary in the ordinary.
6. The place stimulates your senses—you like the way it smells and the sounds that you hear, and it is visually appealing to you.
7. When you're there, you feel as if life is complete. You want for nothing more, because everything you need is right there.
8. You appreciate everything.
9. You experience a feeling of freedom—from intrusive thoughts, tension, and worry.
10. Your creativity flows! You are able to dream, fantasize, and experience *Aha!* moments with ease.
11. Your interactions with others seem friendlier and more fun.

Yes, I know that's eleven. Being able to release your need for perfection and just go with the flow is another sign that you're in a favorite place. And that was twelve. You are less worried about time. Now that's a baker's dozen!

So much of our everyday experience at work is determined by our mind-set. We can be part of the evolution toward a more optimistic business environment by making intentional choices about how we view our circumstances. I'm reminded of a cartoon that I love by motivational speaker and cartoonist, Mike Moore. It shows a prisoner leaning up against the bars of his cell, his hands grasping the bars. The caption reads: "It helps if I look at this as a gated community."

As for Dawson, there are laws that have made it prohibitively difficult for Dawson to be able to travel about freely—so he creates his favorite place right where he is.

Weekly Practice

> *Choose a favorite place that you can get to on your lunch break and visit it two times or more per week. Observe if there are any shifts in how you experience your work time afterward or even before.*

Selected Resources

Korpela, Kalevi Mikael, PhD, and Matti P Yien, MPsych. "Effectiveness of favorite-place prescriptions—A field experimen.t" *American Journal of Preventive Medicine*, 36(5), May 2009, pp. 435-438.

Perseverance

Look at a stone cutter hammering away at his rock,
perhaps a hundred times without as much as a crack showing in it.
Yet at the hundred-and-first blow it will split in two,
and I know it was not the last blow that did it,
but all that had gone before.

—Jacob A. Riis

"Isa-*dooooor*-a. It's time to wake up, sweetie."

It was my second year participating in the annual primate physicals at Frisky's. To make the process less stressful, every monkey had to receive general anesthesia before the physical could be completed. This year I had the honor of holding Isadora, a female black-and-white capuchin monkey, who looks just like Ross's monkey, Marcel, from the television show *Friends.* I was to hold her until the anesthesia started to wear off, and return her to her enclosure just before she started to show "too much attitude." She had been out for a good hour longer than usual this year, and her breathing seemed labored.

Dr. Michael Cranfield, DVM and director for animal health at the Maryland Zoo in Baltimore, and Dr. Keith Gold, DVM, of Chadwell Animal Hospital in Abingdon, Maryland, had finished the last of the twenty-three primate physicals that had begun several hours before. They came up to the recovery room to relax for a few moments and chat with the volunteers before making their final rounds.

While they were in the recovery room, the unthinkable happened. Isadora stopped breathing. I yelled across the room to Dr. Cranfield, "Isadora's not breathing!" My voice was filled with fear, and I think I might have stopped breathing as well, just to keep from having a meltdown. Dr. Cranfield whisked Isadora out of my arms and laid her out flat on the floor. He quickly swung her arms up above her head. I heard a dreadful gasp of air being expelled from her lungs. The next breath *in* never came.

Dr. Cranfield didn't waste a second scooping her up and racing with her back to the infirmary. Dr. Gold was right behind him, along with his two assistants, who had been about to leave for the evening. They dropped their bags and ran back to the infirmary right behind them. Together, the team worked for the next hour, keeping Isadora constantly moving by manually exercising her arms and her legs for her. I watched it all from a video monitor in another room.

Isadora and me

And then they stopped. Isadora lay still. I found myself reverting to my old pleading way of prayer, begging "Please God, no. She's only an adolescent. Don't take her yet."

The team began again. They worked for another half hour. And then I saw it. Isadora's head moved slightly, and her eyes opened. That night Isadora went home with Dr. Gold for observation.

The next morning, Frisky's number showed up on my caller ID. My heart skipped a beat. I picked up quickly and answered with uncertainty in my voice. "Well," said Colleen, "Isadora is back and just finished a blueberry pancake breakfast."

Thank God for perseverance. Whether in our personal lives or in the workplace, it's our ability to act in the face of seemingly overwhelming odds that can create astounding results. Often, it's our conscious decision to choose optimism that gives us the will to persevere.

In a newsletter I received from Sauber and Associates, the speaker, consultant, facilitator, and author, Iris Sauber, writes about the power of persevering through rejection:

> Rejection is a natural aspect of the sales process so don't take it personally. Learn from rejection, use it as a feedback mechanism and look for ways to improve your presentation. Salespeople who take rejection personally lack perseverance and seldom make the sale. Sales is a numbers game pure and simple. As a professional baseball player, if you can average four hits out of ten times at bat you are heading for the Hall of Fame. Research indicates that in sales you can expect your prospect to say NO five times before he or she buys. With this in mind, realize that with every sales rejection you receive, you are one step closer to making the sale!

Thomas Edison said something similar: "Many of life's failures are men who did not realize how close they were to success when they gave up." It took Edison thousands of trials before the light bulb was invented. About his numerous efforts, he said, "I have not failed. I've just found 10,000 ways that won't work."

I thank you, God, for the Thomas Edisons, Dr. Cranfields, and Dr. Golds of the world. Without them, I would not have light at the flick of a switch—or the light that fills my heart whenever I look at Isadora.

Weekly Practice

> *One of my dear teachers taught that it was okay to be a beginner. If you want to be successful at it, "Just do it a thousand times." Notice where you are a beginner. At what do you need to persevere in order to see desired results?*

Selected Resources

Sauber, Iris, Sauber and Associates, LLC. Received in an emailed newsletter from Iris approximately October 2007. www.sauberaa.com.

Quit Complaining!

When a milestone is conquered, the subtle erosion called entitlement begins its consuming grind. The team regards its greatness as a trait and a right. Halfhearted effort becomes habit and saps a champion.

—Pat Riley

At Frisky's, you can tell what time of evening it is by a noise. Bimbee, a weeper capuchin monkey, starts banging a stainless steel spoon against the bars of her enclosure as if to say, "It's eight o'clock. Where's my frozen yogurt and fruit? Let's pick up the pace around here! Can't you people move any faster?" We just know that's what she's tapping out with her spoon. She's grown accustomed to her evening treat and gets downright righteous about it when it's late!

Bimbee

Unlike humans, monkeys don't know how to accommodate the things that throw off their usual feeding schedule, just as they don't understand the need to forgive when things go awry. In July 2008, Baltimore was privileged to receive a visit from Dr. Fred Luskin, internationally acclaimed forgiveness expert and author of *Forgive For Good.* Dr. Luskin shared his "9-Step Forgiveness Intervention" and many other gems of knowledge and heartfelt wisdom. I have pages full of notes from his presentation, and I will paraphrase here the points that struck me the most:

> We live in an "entitlement" culture. One way to fool ourselves is to think that people *owe* us. The truth is, *nobody* owes us a damn thing!
>
> Because so many feel "entitled," people often are not thinking about how to be kind to others. We are all waiting for someone to be kind to *us.* It is what makes the beauty of someone doing something kind for us so profound!
>
> We live in a world where two billion people don't have running water. If you have a hundred dollars in the bank, you have more resources than the majority of the people on the planet. Abraham Maslow, a psychologist who was best known for his conceptualization of the "hierarchy of human needs," said in the early 70s, "I am surprised at how little gratitude I see in a country that is free, relatively safe, and so full of opportunity."

Dr. Luskin told his listeners about a study done at the University of Chicago in which 180 people were asked to wear beepers that had been set to go off several times throughout the day. When the beeper sounded, each participant was to record what he or she was feeling and thinking at the time. The results were astounding: 75 percent of the time, people were complaining—spending a full three-quarters of their time focusing on what was wrong. In Dr. Luskin's opinion, the simplest tool to fix this is gratitude. When we focus on what's *right* and what we're grateful for, the tendency to complain dissipates.

In an online article about complaining at work, author Tom Richard lays it on the line:

> Quit whining about the duties you are asked to do that aren't listed in your job description. If you truly want to become a more valuable businessperson, you must learn to get over your silly self and do more than you are paid for. As Napoleon Hill says, "The man who does more than he is paid for will soon be paid for more than he does."
>
> YOU are the only one who has the power to change the value you provide for others, and the ability to increase the rewards you receive for that value. Do your job well and be proud of the service you provide. When you're mediocre, your results will remain mediocre; but when you're valuable, your rewards will be great!

Chief Happiness Officer, Alexander Kjerulf, author and expert on creating happiness at work, says that complaining becomes a habit. "The more you complain, the easier it gets. In the end, everything is bad, every situation is a problem, every co-worker is a jerk, and nothing is good."

Is it typical for primates, both human and nonhuman, to complain? Bimbee uses her spoon to make loud, distracting noises. We use our tongues to make loud, distracting noises. Isn't that what a complaint is?

The choice for optimism is ours to make. To break the habit of pessimism—and that's all it is, a habit—look for what is right. Gratitude attracts more things for which to be grateful.

Bimbee, that tapping is getting on my nerves—*and* you are so darn cute!

Weekly Practice

> *For this week's practice, you are invited to follow the example of the study participants at the University of Chicago—with a few tweaks to help you choose optimism. Just as in the study, set a beeper or*

*alarm to go off several times each day for the next week. When it does, notice what you are thinking and feeling, and jot it down in your journal. If what you've just jotted down is a complaint, add the word "*and*" after it, and then record something that is* right *about the situation or person you are complaining about.*

Selected Resources

Kjerulf, Alexander. *Happy Hour is 9 to 5*. Accessed online 4/12/11 at http://positivesharing.com/2007/08/top-10-reasons-why-constant-complaining-is-so-toxic-in-the-workplace/

Richard, Tom. "Complaining About Work? Here's the One Change You Need!" Accessed online7/8/10 at http://ezinearticles.com/?Complaining-About-Work?-Heres-the-One-Change-You-Need!&id=152516

Privilege

Do not regret growing older.
It is a privilege denied to many.

—Unknown wise person

Although there are certainly exceptions, it's my observation that most monkeys do not like having their enclosures cleaned. They experience it as a complete invasion of their personal space and belongings. In order for a human to clean the space, the monkey must be denied access to it while "the housekeeper" is in there cleaning it. At Frisky's, each monkey enclosure has both an indoor and an outdoor space. The monkeys are free to go back and forth through the tunnel whenever they please—except when one side needs to be cleaned.

Yoo

Now, I don't know about you, but I have always considered cleaning, lawn mowing, weeding, sweeping the driveway, and window washing to be among the responsibilities of being a homeowner. One hot summer morning, I arrived at Frisky's just as Colleen had filled a bucket with warm water, dish soap, and several rags. I watched as she handed one of the rags to little Yoo, a female weeper capuchin monkey who was born as a preemie and is to this day still petite, but very healthy. Colleen also handed rags to Johnny, Willie, and Babee. While these three took the rags from Colleen and did various things with them, Yoo enthusiastically began cleaning! She went over to the Plexiglas tunnel door that separates the two areas of her enclosure and began washing it. She then took the rag over to the bars and began washing them. She treated this cleaning as if it were a privilege.

In *Mastering Life's Energies*, author Maria Nemeth writes about a conversation she had with a man who was attending one of her workshops. On a break, he told her that he would never forget his father's words, spoken when the older man was near death. His father told him that all his life, he had thought of mowing the grass, taking out the trash, making repairs, and other household tasks as *responsibilities*. He said, "Now, as I lie here, unable to walk and soon to die, I see them as privileges." (pp. 217–218) How privileged we are is most often not in our awareness.

In 2003, I made a commitment to be physically present at Frisky's every Thursday to help with whatever needed to be done. I wanted to deepen my understanding of our human connection with all the other earthlings. In my time at Frisky's, I have had the privilege of giving a second chance at life to hundreds of beings every year.

I know privilege when I am cleaning out the cage of a rabbit whose owner decided not to care for him anymore. It gives my soul joy to let the rabbit out into a play area, where he can feel the earth beneath his feet while I clean the feces from his cage.

I know privilege when I hold a baby squirrel in my hand while feeding it, and then providing bowel and bladder encouragement to keep it from suffering a blockage and dying. That encouragement is usually the mother's task; in her absence, the babies would die without the help.

No one should have to sit in his own feces. No one should die because his body is not yet physically capable of releasing waste. No one should be abandoned or given up on. To be able to watch another life thrive because of my interaction is a true privilege.

George Bernard Shaw offers his view on privilege in the following quotation. It captures the essence of what I feel in my heart about my time at Frisky's Wildlife and Primate Sanctuary:

> This is the true joy in life, the being used for a purpose recognized by yourself as a mighty one; the being a force of nature instead of a feverish selfish clod of ailments and grievances complaining that the world will not devote itself to making you happy. I am of the opinion that my life belongs to the whole community and as long as I live it is my privilege to do for it whatever I can. I want to be thoroughly used up when I die, for the harder I work, the more I live. I rejoice in life for its own sake. Life is no "brief candle" to me. It is a sort of splendid torch which I have a hold of for the moment, and I want to make it burn as brightly as possible before handing it over to future generations.

Weekly Practice

As this book comes to a close, I invite you to ponder with me two final questions:

Where can I shift my thinking away from responsibility and toward seeing my actions in life as a privilege?

Where can you, in the workplace, take the rag like little Yoo and know the privilege inherent in having the work to do and the ability to serve?

Selected Resources

Nemeth, Maria, PhD. *Mastering Life's Energies.* p. 217–218. Novato, CA: New World Library, 2007.

Shaw, George Bernard, Irish playwright (July 26, 1856–November 2, 1950). Quote accessed online 2/27/12 at http://www.arvinddevalia.com/

In Memory

Remembering all those who have touched our lives and gone before us ...

You will get the essence of these lovely earthlings as you read their stories.

Patsy

Rhesus macaque monkey, female

Born April 15, 1985, died August 26, 2006

Scotty, Jr.

Vervet guenon monkey, male

Born October 3, 1995, died July 17, 2009

Squeaky

Gothic squirrel monkey, male

Born August 14, 1988, died August 21, 2007

Nicole

Gothic squirrel monkey, female

Born December 15, 1985, died March 15, 2006

Rachelle

Rhesus macaque monkey, female

Born June 6, 1992, died April 5, 2006

Zoey

Bolivian squirrel monkey, female

Born April 30, 1994, died May 2, 2008

Sam

Blue guenon monkey, male

Born July 15, 1984, died February 9, 2006

Mr. Bojangles

Java macaque Monkey, male

Born Spring 1986, died August 22, 2001

Bimbee

Weeper capuchin monkey, female

Born September 15, 1971, died July 14, 2011

Cindy Lou

Gothic squirrel monkey, female

Born September 15, 1991, died December 7, 2011

Unwanted, abandoned pets ...
Injured, orphaned, displaced wildlife ...
Giving them all a second chance.

Frisky's Wildlife and Primate Sanctuary, Inc.

Frisky's Wildlife and Primate Sanctuary, Inc. is a 501(c)3 nonprofit organization. Frisky's receives no county, state, or federal funding. Nobody receives a paycheck for their work at Frisky's, and there are no fees charged for services. It is a completely volunteer-run organization. Frisky's depends on the good-hearted donations from the public.

If you would like to help Frisky's to continue its mission, you can donate online at www.friskys.org or by mailing a check to:

Frisky's Wildlife and Primate Sanctuary, Inc.
10790 Old Frederick Road/ Rt. 99
Woodstock, MD 21163

A portion of the sales price of every copy of this book will be donated to Frisky's Wildlife and Primate Sanctuary, Inc.

Open Book Editions
A Berrett-Koehler Partner

Open Book Editions is a joint venture between Berrett-Koehler Publishers and Author Solutions, the market leader in self-publishing. There are many more aspiring authors who share Berrett-Koehler's mission than we can sustainably publish. To serve these authors, Open Book Editions offers a comprehensive self-publishing opportunity.

A Shared Mission

Open Book Editions welcomes authors who share the Berrett-Koehler mission—Creating a World That Works for All. We believe that to truly create a better world, action is needed at all levels—individual, organizational, and societal. At the individual level, our publications help people align their lives with their values and with their aspirations for a better world. At the organizational level, we promote progressive leadership and management practices, socially responsible approaches to business, and humane and effective organizations. At the societal level, we publish content that advances social and economic justice, shared prosperity, sustainability, and new solutions to national and global issues.

Open Book Editions represents a new way to further the BK mission and expand our community. . We look forward to helping more authors challenge conventional thinking, introduce new ideas, and foster positive change.

For more information, see the Open Book Editions website:
http://www.iuniverse.com/Packages/OpenBookEditions.aspx

Join the BK Community! See exclusive author videos, join discussion groups, find out about upcoming events, read author blogs, and much more! http://bkcommunity.com/